YOUR HOME

YOUR SANCTUARY

CLODAGH

WRITTEN WITH HEATHER RAMSDELL

PHOTOGRAPHY BY DANIEL AUBRY

CLODAGH

Rizzoli
NEW YORK

DEDICATION

TO DANIEL AUBRY, MY HUSBAND, WHO IS MY HOME AND MY SANCTUARY.

First published in the United States of America in 2008
by Rizzoli International Publications, Inc.
300 Park Avenue South
New York, New York 10010
www.rizzoliusa.com

Text copyright © 2008 Clodagh
Photography copyright © 2008 Daniel Aubry

2008 2009 2010 2011 / 10 9 8 7 6 5 4 3 2 1

Printed in China

ISBN-13: 978-0-8478-3160-9

Library of Congress Catalog Control Number:
2008928757

Project Editor: Sandra Gilbert
Designer: Ivette Montes de Oca, Overlap Design
Production: Kaija Markoe and Walter de la Vega

Prop Credit: page 24 Invitation, courtesy of Printicon,
New York

A portion of my proceeds from this book will go to Clodagh
Cares, a philanthropic charity for food and education
for children in emerging countries.

ACKNOWLEDGMENTS

Special thanks to the book team: architectural and interior photographer, Daniel Aubry; writers Heather Ramsdell and Daniel DeClerico; coordinators Heather O'Neill, Jill Cohen, Louis Monaco, and Rebecca Edmondson; book designer Ivette Montes de Oca; copy editor Lynn Scrabis; and editor Sandy Gilbert and Rizzoli for believing in this project.

My sincere thanks to all of those involved in making this book a reality:

Alan Swanson, Alexandra De Gedeon, Alexandra Denise Castro, Alison Stewart, Amneris Rasuk, Amy Lee, Amy Levin, Ana Goldstein-Kogan, Andrea Panico, Ashley Hermann, Beverly Watson Matos, Bill Burns, Bonnie Lunt, Brendan Keim, Caroline Rippeteau, Carolyn Hagan, Christian "Andy" Pizzarro, Christopher Ventresca, Claudia Colantonio, Conni Evans, Craig Solomon, Dana Rudys, Daniel Gabrielli, Daniel J. Moore, Daniel Pontius, DaShawn Pretlow, Delta Wright, Diana Schrage, Dianne Quander, Donnalynn Civello, Elena Frampton, Elisabeth de Morentin, Emily Vanderveen, Enrique Limon, Eric Alley, Eric Anderson, Erica Skelly, Espen Eiborg, Eve Coleman, Eve Suter, Flavia Portugal, Gilles-fleur Boutry, Gita Nandan, Gloria Saavedra, Graham Bigelow, Greg Guity, Harry King, Hassan Spruill, Hilary Gilford, Hillary Gregga, Huy Bui, Ilene Shaw, Jack Lenor Larsen, Jackie Bourke, Jane Newman, Janna Sabalakova, Jay Heubert, Jeffrey Cheng, Jenn Diamond, Jennifer DiLeonardi, Jeremy Ortman, Jessica Lo, Jill Grunberger, John Henderson, Julie Babin, Julie Stahl

PREVIOUS PAGE
A door sets up anticipation for what happens next. The dark copper of this door is rich and inviting. A custom door-pull was cast using the abstract of local camellia flowers. Fixed glass panels on either side of the door are set on the same plane as the outdoor deck to bring the outside in and the inside out. The glass banding casts shadows and sunlight on the floor of the interior.

OPPOSITE
Outdoor fabrics used indoors are great for their stain resistance, fending off the wear of pets, children, and the occasional toppled glass of wine. African mud huts inspired this indoor/outdoor textile by Perennials, a solution-dyed acrylic that's durable enough to withstand a bleach sponging to take off deep-set red-wine stains. Besides being easy to clean, low maintenance materials are more sustainable than fragile ones.

Juliette Spencer, Karen Fisher, Kate Verner, Katie Miller, Katryna Carter, Kelsey Harrington, Kim Harris, Kim-Marie Ugenti, Kristan Klassen, Larah Moravek, Laura Farrell, Leeann Brzozowski, Lindsay Parrish, Liza Behles, Madeline Chang, Maine Smith, Marcela Perez, Margo Krasne, Marilien Romme, Marjorie Lipman-Lipari, Mary Luria, Marybeth Raymond, Mia Bourke, Mike Strohl, Miloika Penon, Missy Renard, Myrna DeJesus, Nancie Min, Nathalie Droulers, Nelson Barreto, Niall Smith, Nina Abrams, Paula Tancock Burrell, Peter O'Kennedy, Peter Oudejans, Rachel Wood Massey, Rafique Francis, Regan Billingsley, Richard Rodelo, Robert Chia & Associates, Robert Pierpont, Sarah Moylan, Seema Shah, Sergio Mercado, Shannon Ulis, Siobhan McDonald, Steffani Aarons, Stephen O'Kennedy, Susie Hoffmann, Tadashi Matsuda, Tal Geller, Terri Carr Erdos, Than Hansen, Tim O'Kennedy, Todd Capron, Todd Coleman, Todd Henderson, Tomio Nagaoka, Ute Guenther, Valerie Aubry, Veranica Komin, Willy Gahungu, Yan Bourke, Yolanda do Campo, Yvette Feinberg, and to all my colleagues and clients past, present, and future.

OPPOSITE
Art is the focus in this matte-white plastered entry gallery. The client commissioned this thirteen-foot-wide Marco Tirelli painting. It is installed over cold-rolled steel benches that can be pulled up to the dining room table for extra seating. This entrance represents the earth elements and conveys the owner's love of *wabi-sabi*. Wide-board reclaimed-walnut floors echo the message of sustainability.

FOLLOWING PAGE
This quiet corridor is "living" LOHAS, short for Lifestyle of Health and Sustainability. A parade of flickering long-lasting LED candles mounted on steel bases bring good feng shui through positive kinetic energy. Reclaimed-wood slats hide mechanical systems in the ceiling; when the systems need to be serviced or maintained, the slats are easy to take down temporarily.

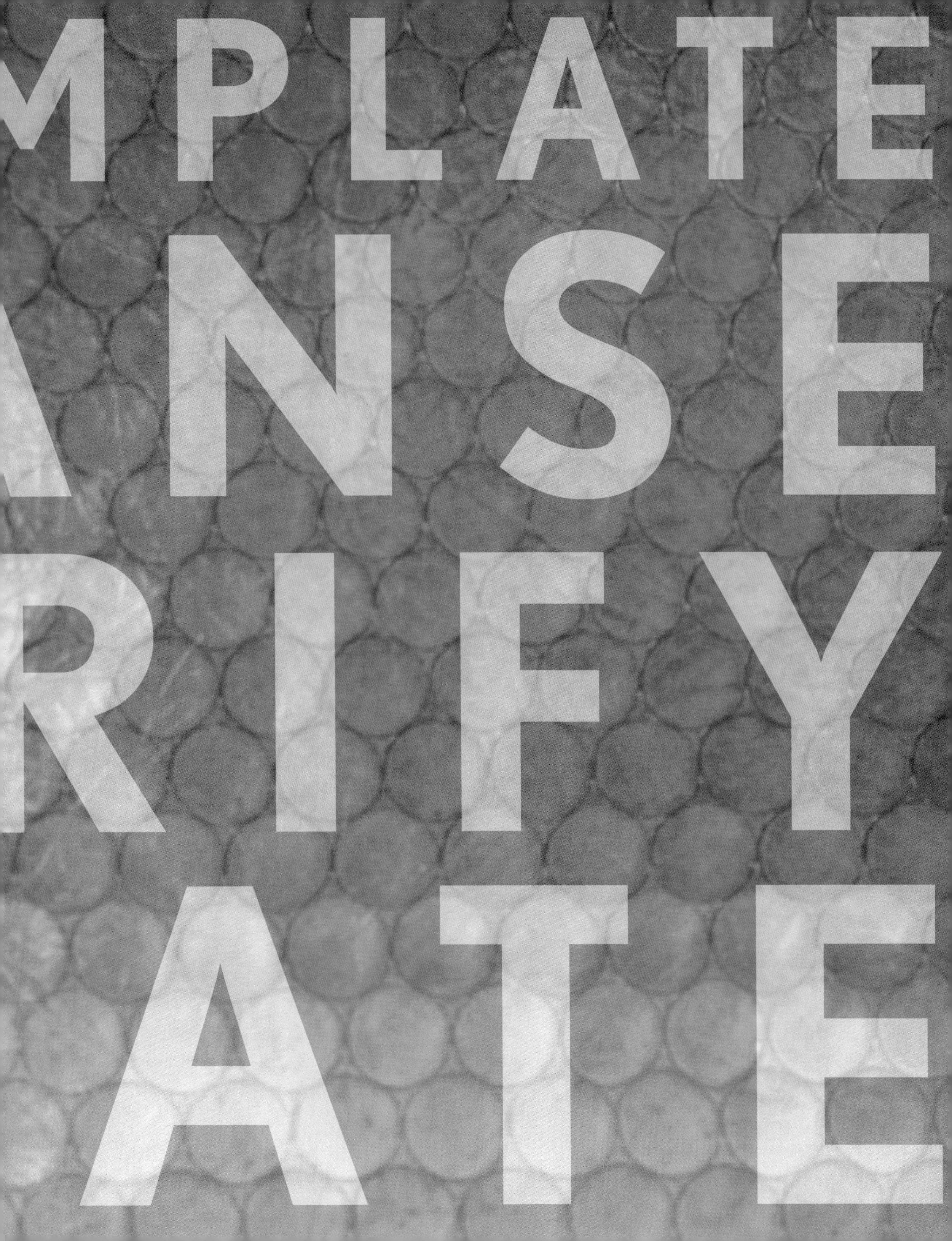
MPLATE
ANSE
RIFY
ATE

YOUR HOME, YOUR SANCTUARY

There are many things that make us human, from rational thought to opposable thumbs, but in my view what defines us most is the extent to which we're shaped by our surroundings. Consider the feeling you get when you walk into a harmonious room, compared to one that's visually noisy and frenetic. You'll be able to adapt to either setting, but one will calm your nerves while the other will fray them.

Whether you spend every free moment at home or just alight there between trips to rejuvenate, your home is the surrounding that defines you most powerfully and completely. My goal as a designer has always been to create spaces that transcend their material properties to fulfill human needs, so that occupants can realize the most vivid, joyful version of themselves. To accomplish this, it is necessary to design more than just the physical space. Just as a visit to a spa provides a haven from stress and public chaos, your home should take care of you, calm you, and leave you refreshed. The sense of your home as sanctuary should envelop you before you even enter the front door. A true sanctuary is sustainable, sensual, sexy, and serene. When you finally arrive there, you should breathe a sigh of relief and think, "Ahhh, I'm home."

I think of design and architecture not just as disciplines but also as healing arts that support the spirit as well as the body. The comments I hope to hear when people move into spaces I've designed are "Our lives are richer," "We work together better as a family," and "I feel more relaxed." More than the standard, "It looks great," or "I like the furniture," this feedback tells me that I've done my job.

The point of *Your Home, Your Sanctuary* is, first and foremost, to persuade you of the importance of having a home that supports you in every way, and then to share my ideas for creating it. It's taken me several months to put these thoughts to paper, but really I've been compiling them my entire life. This book is a way to convey all that I've learned, for you to absorb, practice, and pass along to the next person. Remember, there's no such thing as a savings account for ideas, or knowledge, or love. Plus the more you share, the more opportunity you'll have for new discoveries. And sharing may be the most human act of all.

START HERE

Turning your home into a sanctuary requires some work and thought. Take a careful inventory of the way you live, and consider the way you wish to live. Clarity in the rooms of your home translates to clarity of mind. Rooms need to be cleared of clutter to present clarity and sources of joy. I'm a firm believer in feng shui, the ancient Chinese art of placement whereby homes are seen as direct extensions of the people who live in them. If you have a messy house, your life will also be messy. But through the careful application of colors and materials (or elements, as they're known in the philosophy), you'll create a harmonious home, and that energy will suffuse your mind and body. The balancing act requires constant attention, but in the same way that regular exercise is essential to physical health, the more thought you invest in your home, the more it will support you. These ten questions, and the ideas in the pages that follow, will set the wheels in motion for you. I would not dare attempt to teach you who you are, but rather to try to clear a path for you to discover yourself. To begin, find a pen and a notebook, at least twenty minutes of free time, and someplace to sit by yourself. Turn off your phone. Then ask yourself these questions about your home:

- Is it harmonious and balanced?

- Does it enhance my life and bring me joy?

- Does my heart lift with pleasure when I think about it?

- Is it comfortable?

- Is there stagnation and clutter?

- Are the sounds there soothing?

- Is it a place for healing and wellness?

- Can I invite anyone there at any time without stress?

- Can guests open my closet doors without me feeling embarrassed?

- Do I get upset when I think about it? If so, what are the problems?

Listen to your gut for honest answers, and then, with these pages as a guide, begin to plot the necessary changes.

PREVIOUS PAGE
Reclaimed wood forms the chunky ebonized steps floating on steel stair stringers. Slender steel members topped by a hammered steel handrail are sturdy and supportive. A chalky line drawing animates the gray-beige plaster.

OPPOSITE
Lighting is used to correct the feng shui of a long gallery. Stainless steel ceiling lamps illuminate the artwork and are counter balanced by recessed floor lights, animating the *chi* behind the columns.

FOLLOWING PAGES
Left: An eighteen-foot stretch of walnut makes a dining table for twenty. Right: This biophilia-inspired designed carpet was produced by Bentley Prince Street. Its pattern is based on the light and shadow of branches.

PARTY
YO
HO

You enter your home. The moment you close the front door, shutting out the exterior sounds and stresses, your shoulders relax, your breathing quiets, and if the space supports it, your energies align. Welcome to your sanctuary. The sense of balance and harmony that your home provides should start with the front door. A familiar scent, whether lavender, lemon, or sandalwood, along with ample lighting, will trigger an instant feeling of security. Configure the entryway correctly, and when it's time to go out again, you'll leave feeling vibrant and renewed.

HELLO, GOOD-BYE

Just as every person has a face every home has a front door. You have only one chance to make a first impression with your home: what happens in the few feet around the doorway itself makes all the difference. Depending on how your entry is appointed, the transition will feel open or congested, welcoming or oppressive. Either way, the impression is lasting—not just for guests but for you as well, every time you come and go.

Even before you reach the front door, you begin processing the feel of a home; for example, you might notice if a neat pathway clearly indicates where the entrance is. Then when you reach the door, you perceive the roof overhead providing protection from the elements. These subtle cues add up to create a sense of invitation.

Your impressions will continue after passing through the front door into the foyer. Designed properly, an entry space sets the tone for the rest of the home. Look for ways to visually prepare the eye for what's to come; for example, with an object of nature or art that is beautiful to you. The foyer must serve a practical purpose as well, offering a bench to rest on, a mirror for last-minute touch-ups, or a console table with a dish for keys and the daily mail. The exit is a similar process but in reverse, safely ushering you or your guests out into the surprises of the day.

PREVIOUS PAGE
Tufa red artisan plaster is framed by an ancient, partially stripped brick arch. Graphite river stones line the wall and an abstract landscape painting is placed for feng shui to imply depth and more space. The cushy bench provides literal support. In terms of sustainability, the plaster has a lifetime guarantee and the original maple floors were cleaned and resealed. Over-whelming baseboards were removed and replaced by the horizontal baseboard of the river stones.

OPPOSITE
At the end of a corridor of hand-combed mulberry and silver closet doors, an eighteenth-century wooden medicine Buddha sits on a hand-hammered chunk of stone, backlit by a reflective gold-leaf wall. The message is one of kindness and joy. The master bedroom door is to the left. A study suite to the right can be totally independent from the rest of the apartment or double doors can be opened to unite the space.

ENTRY ESSENTIALS

LIGHTING

Low illumination along an exterior pathway and a beautiful sconce mounted next to the door will make visitors feel welcome. Alternatively, a simple overhead fixture can create a pool of light that is as effective as a welcome mat at indicating the entry point. Put hallway lights on a dimmer switch. The glow is festive and flattering, especially for entertaining.

AROMA

Like animals, we sniff subliminally as we approach a home. A fresh-baked pie, a citrus candle, and lavender cleaning wax—all conjure up the right impressions. If these delicious scents seep out from the entry door, you'll be conditioned before you enter to expect warmth and intimacy. Stale air has the opposite effect, leading visitors to anticipate an atmosphere of stagnation inside.

THE PATH

A clearly defined path is the start of a tranquil journey into your home. It might begin with an ornate gate that swings out over stone pavers bordered by a fragrant lawn, or it may be a narrow pebble trail that crunches deliciously underfoot with each step. Remember, it's difficult to erase a bad impression from your psyche as you come and go.

KEY DROP

The door should open with a smooth turn of the key. If your lock does not open easily, get it fixed right away. Cranky locks create cranky people. Always keep keys in the same spot just inside the entry, so that you know instinctively where to find them; time spent frantically searching for these everyday items is lost for good.

THE FRONT DOOR

The front door sets the stage for what goes on behind it. Some doors are as blank as the visage of a poker player; others are statements of pure emotion, with burnished metal and ancient wood. Make sure the door complements your home's architectural style. If it suits your fancy, include an unexpected feature, such as a glass transom or metal mesh view panel.

FOCUS

Upon entering your home, your eye should rest on something meaningful. Create a focal point around an object that you love; it will speak to you every time you enter, so make sure you like what it says. A fresh-cut flower on a simple console table offers a perfect tableau. Like a Japanese *tokonoma*, it celebrates the senses and offers a silent welcome.

STORAGE

A little bit of order will go a long way toward maintaining serenity in the home. Coats should go immediately into a closet, so they don't end up slung over the backs of kitchen chairs. Briefcases belong in the home office area; shoes should be put away. If you entertain often and don't have spare closet space, roll out a portable rack with hangers for guests.

MESSAGES

Written messages still have their place in the home. A magnet on a metal door can hold a reminder, or you might consider mounting a chalkboard to the wall beside the entry, especially one leading into a mudroom. Instructions for visitors can be conveyed simply through visual prompts: for example, a bench with a row of slippers indicates that this is a shoes-off household.

WATER, REFLECTION, AND SOUND

The sound of water splashing on stones, the space-expanding power of a well-placed mirror, the music of wind chimes: use these elements to create positive feng shui at your home's entry. A mirror also allows you to check yourself as you come and go; a full-length one will give you a complete view and also encourage you to stand up straight.

KEYS TO A SERENE ENTRY

AVOID ABRUPT TRANSITIONS. The main entry door should not open directly onto the living space. However, if this is how the space is built, delineate an entry area in front of the door using color, different flooring, lighting, a console table, an area rug, or a "wall" of floor plants. Establishing a clear threshold between the outside world and the interior one will allow visitors to slough off their public personas and relax into their private selves.

BUILD GOOD HABITS. It is easy to treat an entry vestibule as a dumping ground for coats, knapsacks, and other items. Resisting this tendency requires some discipline, but it only takes a few weeks to create a healthy new habit. At the risk of sounding like your mother, train yourself not to jettison your coat and bag when you step through the door. Key drops and coat hooks are truly habit forming.

GIVE YOURSELF VISUAL CUES. Display a beautiful piece of art that has personal meaning in the foyer. This gesture will celebrate the fact that you are the most honored guest in your own residence. By creating a system of order for the entry, tailored to your specific needs, you'll experience serenity every time you come and go.

OPPOSITE
Natural elements in this painting trio soften the transition between indoors and outdoors. The coat hooks, in an anteroom to a glamorous powder room, slot through a long, flat slice of cold-rolled steel and function as storage for guests.

THE FIVE ELEMENTS
EARTH, FIRE, WATER, WOOD, METAL

According to feng shui, it is important to represent each of the five elements to create a balanced room. The elements relate to each other in a cycle of creation and destruction. For example, water generates wood, but douses fire. If one element dominates a space, the energy will be off kilter. It's a careful balancing act, but when done correctly it puts people at ease. The elements tie into the Chinese year of your birth and your birth sign, so certain elements will speak more to you than others. (It's easy to look up your Chinese birth year online.) Each element represents different qualities and is associated with different materials and colors:

Earth (yellow)—caring, supportive, nourishing, family oriented, stability, grounding.

Fire (red)—self-expression, emotional extremes, empathy, desire for attention, sociability, talkativeness.

Water (black)—solitude, privacy, introspection, philosophy, mystery, truth, honesty, anxiety, nervousness, insecurity.

Wood (green)—leadership, assertiveness, creativity, planning, decision-making, competitiveness, conflict, anger, frustration.

Metal (white)—precise, meticulous, logical, analytical, moderation, self-control, morality, pessimism.

(See *Glossary* on page 208 for more about these elements.)

OPPOSITE
The five elements in this entryway are balanced. A concrete fountain resting on a rough-hewn limestone slab welcomes people with the pleasing sound of water splashing over polished river stones. Light represents fire in feng shui. Behind the fountain, a tall screen of acrylic and teak veneer strips glows with natural light during the day and becomes an incandescent light at night.

BEFORE YOU GO

Your entrance welcomes people into your home—but it also sends them on their way when they depart. Try to establish a connection to the outdoors to make the transition a smooth one; for example, you might install stone floor tiles in the foyer that match the material of your front porch. I also often make the inside of the door the same color as the outside. Whatever you do, don't paint the interior of the door the same color as an adjacent closet, or your guests may end up walking in there instead of gracefully exiting to the outside.

Windows are one of my favorite and most valuable design tools, especially for homes that are situated in beautiful settings. They're like nature's picture frames. Similarly, French doors are an excellent way to allow a glimpse to the outside world before you ever step foot from the house.

OPPOSITE
A stone garden with quiet echoes of Japan and a generous protected entryway welcome guests to a home that celebrates easy living. A bench subtly signals "shoes off" and an abstract landscape painting conveys the owners' love of art. Out of the frame of this photograph a fountain splashes and gurgles.

FOLLOWING PAGES
Left: A vertical poem of rods graces the corner of a studio; ancient twisted vines mingle with Tuareg tent posts and tai chi sticks. Right: A closet with four louvered doors above a shoes-off bench provides outerwear storage. Louvers allow outerwear to breathe and dry. Four pools of light cascade down as much to please the eye as to illuminate the area.

When most people hear the word sanctuary, they often think of a quiet, solitary space. But sanctuaries can be rich, energizing, communal areas too, provided their energy is balanced and harmonious. My design projects almost always call for one of these large, busy gathering places where families and friends can congregate for laughter, celebration, games, and entertainment. Even during hard times, a common room provides a safe haven for family members to take comfort in one anothers' company.

TALKING, PLAYING, SOCIALIZING, LOUNGING, EATING, KISSING

The secret to planning a common room is flexibility. Furniture plays a vital role in supporting the diverse range of activities that take place there. Start by bringing in the largest dining table the space will allow; its mere presence will send a signal that this room is all about people being social. Next, carve up the open floor plan with area rugs; for example, you might use a rug to define an entertainment center in one section, with a large, cozy sofa that the family can gather on to watch movies or read. When organizing a large space, it's also helpful to think about focal points, such as a stone fireplace or a large picture window. If the common room borders the kitchen, an island countertop might offer a focus as well, especially during parties when it is the site of a gorgeous buffet.

It is important to be mindful of feng shui in the common room because so much activity takes place there. The room should contain a harmonious balance of all five elements: earth (stone or concrete), water (if you don't have a water view, artwork representing water will do), fire (a fireplace), wood (furniture or flooring), and metal (a lamp). Bright tones, especially orange, encourage communication and interaction. As for the layout, maintain an even number of seats and group furniture to allow space for the flow of people and energy. Provided you are deliberate in your planning of this communal space, anything can work.

PREVIOUS PAGE
A deep sofa in a seating area looks out on a city terrace. The intimate placement of the upholstered pieces encourages conversation. A generous reclaimed-wood coffee table provides a feeling of permanence. Color and texture variations in the natural slate flooring support biophilia.

OPPOSITE
The movement of brilliant tropical fish provides a fun backdrop for this family dinner table. Small children live here, and all of the finishes are childproof. The red of a lacquer Chinese wedding chest stimulates appetite and energetic conversation. In feng shui, healthy fish in clear water bring prosperity, and the use of all colors in the room balances energy and appeals to all tastes.

OPPOSITE

This dining area can be veiled from the owners' kitchen by a stainless steel mesh curtain that slides back into a slot and becomes totally invisible for normal use. The curtain separates the preparation area from the eating area, but both cook and guests can see and hear one another through the mesh. This is a perfect example of defining space without confining it. The children have a homework and breakfast ledge as part of the kitchen.

FOLLOWING PAGES

A queen-size bed, upholstered in the same material as the wall, becomes a deep, curl-up couch where parents and grandparents play with kids or read. Closing the doors on the alcove turns it into a guest suite. The powder room, with a concealed shower, is a perfect guest bath. Stairs lead up to the owners' bedrooms, workspace, and playroom. The patterns in this Armenian rug are inspired by tree bark.

PREVIOUS PAGES
An enormous New York loft offers many places to play, rest, or study. At one end, a raised seating group centered around an amber resin table offers water views. In the middle, an eighteen-foot slice of walnut flanked by steel benches can support dinner for thirty. A media room is made cozier with a deep amber chenille sectional sofa and can be closed off by visored steel doors for daytime movie watching or an extra overnight guest.

OPPOSITE
This corner of an urban common room is designed for casual dining. White faux-leather banquettes wipe down well. The massive table is topped with a cast slab of white concrete that has been sealed against stains. Two leaning, stacked porcelain vases are a light-hearted focal point, and sturdy but airy-looking swivel chairs provide counterpoint.

FOLLOWING PAGES
A structural column bisected this gallery entry in an odd place, so we added another column with an angled slot to create a screen with a framed view. Cold-rolled steel panels line the slot and a matching steel floor grid with a recessed upward pointing light splashes brightness and shadow at night.

COMMON ROOM ESSENTIALS

ENTERTAINMENT

"The rack," as audio-visual zealots call their entertainment equipment, is visually noisy, so do house it in a discreet, built-in storage area. Be sure to hide all the cords. Buy the largest flat screen TV that you can afford, since it will have to entertain a crowd. A karaoke machine, a good piano, and an electronic keyboard are ideal for parties.

INTROSPECTION

You might also use the common room for yoga, tai chi, or simple relaxation. This is why movable furniture or building furniture into walls makes sense: it creates a swathe of floor space to roll out a yoga mat, exercise ball, or prayer stool. If you always meditate in the same spot, your body will start releasing stress as soon as you sit down there.

NOMADIC DINING

Encourage everyday eating in various places: dinner in front of the TV; sushi at the coffee table; Sunday morning pastries on the sofa. Strong wooden stools can function as either seating or tables. Tall stools at the kitchen counter are good for dinner guests or small children. Line a wall with benches, so that there will be extra seating during large buffet-style gatherings.

KITCHEN AREA

Ideally, the kitchen should be part of the common room. No matter where you start a party, it eventually ends up in the kitchen. Why not embrace this fact? If you have an island counter, surround it with high stools for guests to perch upon and sip a drink or coffee. Intimate conversation happens best side-by-side, so this area is a boon to familial communication.

BEAUTY

Sightlines are key in a room that balances so much activity. Place a major life-enhancing artwork in a prominent location. Enormous soft pillows layer in color and texture. If you're at the remodeling stage, create what I call a "slice of wall," Japanese *tokonoma*, or built-in cabinets finished to match the walls that can hide away board games, photo albums, and more.

SCALE

Bigger is better for the common room. A massive sectional sofa is a luxurious invitation to sit; a long console or media center evokes the drama of a limousine. When decorating, remember that overscale art looks best in large spaces. However, small furnishings, such as an intimate card table and chairs, can work in a corner of a large room.

SEATING

Each family member must have a comfortable chair or spot on a sofa. Keep the seating close enough for conversation, and anchor it with a generous coffee table. A pile of large floor pillows can offer flexible seating for half a dozen guests. A window seat is ideal for daydreaming and napping. Good reading lights beside sofas and chairs are imperative.

TABLES

A sturdy, oversized coffee table can act as a place to spread out books or to stage a noisy backgammon contest. Consider drum or oval end tables rather than square or rectangular ones to soften the sharp angles. For large holiday dinners, butt folding tables together and cover them with beautiful textiles or a stretch of a multicolored Kilim rug.

FLEXIBILITY

This room is the hardest-working room in your sanctuary. It needs to function like an inner courtyard where everyone can gather to meet, read, talk, collaborate, watch a movie, drink, and socialize. Imagine this room as a stage for a dozen life plays. Keep the shapes of the furnishings simple, the color harmonious, and the materials easy to maintain.

WINDOWS: LOOKING OUT

People tend to consider windows last when planning their homes. This is a big mistake. Look out your window. What do you see? At the site-planning phase, it's possible to frame a stately elm tree or other striking view. Windows are the eyes of the home, yet many people veil them with treatments that are reminiscent of old-fashioned hoop skirts—Austrian shades, heavy drapes, valances. These are fantastic for storing dust mites, but not for dressing up a window. Instead, consider simple wooden blinds or roller shades, both of which have clean lines and allow natural light to filter into the room. A window might be the only architectural element in a small room, so celebrate it. Moon windows or tiny fixed windows that frame a piece of landscape or sky are live art. If you have no private outdoor space, create depth by planting a window box on the interior and something else in a box on the outside sill. This layering will establish a connection between the indoors and outdoors. A window can also provide great natural theater if you frame the view with a bird feeder or melodious wind chimes.

Whenever possible, I love to include window seats in common rooms. Next time you enter a room with one of these features, see if you aren't instantly drawn to it. As with any enclosed space, window seats provide a sense of security, like curling up in a secret hiding place when we were children. The expansive views they offer of the exterior world, meanwhile, have a healing effect. There's an expression in biophilia, "shelter and savannah," whereby one is looking out from a shelter onto an open plain. For me, window seats capture this balance perfectly.

OPPOSITE
Cushioned window seats deep enough to lie on are upholstered in tactile blue gray. Built-in seating grounds a room and energizes windows that are often at an uncomfortable height. They also beckon owners to enjoy an hour with a good book and offer a view of the outside.

IMPORTANT INDULGENCES

LET NOSTALGIA BE A GUIDE WHEN DECORATING. Before deciding on a color palette for this room, meditate on the places that made you feel good in the past. A color will often attend this memory. Use it as inspiration for choosing the room's palette, as well as the list of materials, including fabrics, wall treatments, and flooring. Although a monochromatic color scheme keeps a room's energy in balance, every color in the spectrum should be reflected in some small way.

SET UP A BAR. A place to open a bottle of wine or mix up a few margaritas so that drinks can be served without going into the kitchen is a good thing to have. Keep snacks like nuts and chocolates there in a refrigerated drawer, and have a second chamber full of cold beers, sodas, and other beverages, as well as an ice drawer.

USE THE FIREPLACE. If you can afford it and have the space, on cold days there is nothing better to gather around than a crackling fireplace. Wood-burning fireplaces are more atmospheric, but gas units are easier to retrofit to your home. Not everyone can have a fireplace, so luckily the kitchen substitutes as an emotional hearth.

OPPOSITE
The concrete hearth is ample enough to be used to place cushions for extra seating. A soaring stucco chimney wall pierced by a steel firebox stirs primeval feelings of gathering and the joy of storytelling. The root *chakra* is the color of fire and energizes the other six *chakras*. This hearth focuses a group of chairs and a sofa that sit on a textured Tufenkian wool rug. The floor is ebonized reclaimed wood.

FOLLOWING PAGES
A massive cast-concrete slab table is the stage for formal dinners or morning coffee. The three-tiered Ingo Maurer paper chandelier hangs well below the doorframe to refract the *chi* in this long room, instead of simply letting it pour out the window. A polished black granite fountain seated on river rocks echoes the owners' love of Japan and adds good *chi* as clean running water promotes prosperity and harmony.

(pages 56-57): This long room catches
the last rays of western sunshine each day.
It is divided into two seating areas: one for
TV and the other for introspection and
conversation. Deep, back-to-back sofas sit
on matching handwoven Armenian rugs.
The room is encircled with small LED lights
to create a curtain of light. Colors are
neutral and rich to ground long views of
water, light, and clouds. Left (page 58): In
the same South Beach high-rise, soft seating
is placed around an overscale ottoman. A
movie lamp has been placed to collect and
diffuse the energy of a sharp angle in the
corner. Right (page 59): Slatted sliding
doors made from Bolivian wood close off a
kitchen. This is a way to enclose space without confining it. Kitchen lights glow through
the slats like a giant Japanese lantern.

OPPOSITE

In this flexible common room in a loft,
translucent sliding doors open and close to
define different areas. The owner can wheel
a big blue ottoman aside and turn one area
into a tai chi room. The ottoman itself is a
queen-size bed and can also be joined to
the sectional for the family to group and
enjoy movies. An artist-painted door with
a handle cast from a mold of oyster sticks
conceals the door of a guest bathroom.

FOLLOWING PAGES

Left (page 62): Wooden beams reclaimed
from a cotton factory form this thirteen-foot
dining table on a sturdy base. An inviting
mingle of upholstered chairs and benches
flank it. An eight-by-eight-foot art light made
from paper collaged on acrylic gives off a
pleasant evening glow. Right (page 63):
A curled piece of found driftwood adds a
layer of texture to this long wooden table.
The quiet design of this table provides the
right backdrop for whatever activity takes
place there, whether it is a raucous dinner
party, a business meeting, or an evening of
homework. (pages 65-66) A walnut dining
table seats twenty. The soul of the tree is
represented in its amazing grain. *Wabi-
sabi* is celebrated in the untouched cracks
and imperfections. Sturdy dining chairs
with slip-cased seats and removable backs
can be dry-cleaned.

The kitchen is the creative center and emotional hearth of the home. I'm referring first and foremost to the preparation of daily nourishment. But this room, where raw ingredients are transformed into delicious meals, is also a laboratory for enduring wellness as the daily ritual of fueling your body stimulates all your senses and feeds your soul. Because the room engages all the senses at once, it's a lush repository for memories. Who can't recall with detailed, nostalgia-filled clarity the kitchen of their youth?

EXPERIMENTING, EATING, TALKING

Give me three minutes alone with your refrigerator and I'll tell you a lot about yourself. Kitchens are emotional spaces, so their planning requires absolute honesty. The more truthful you are about how you'll use this space, the better it will serve you; for example, there's nothing wrong with eating takeout five nights a week, unless your kitchen is designed for daily gourmet cooking and frequent entertaining. If you don't cook, you would want a simpler space.

If you enjoy cooking, you'll have some strategizing to do. Simple, sufficient storage is the one must here. Good habits (or, worse, enduring conflicts) will form around the storage system you devise, so leave nothing to chance. Conduct some careful fact gathering, taking inventory of every cabinet and drawer, and assign a place for each item. Give priority to those utensils and supplies you use most frequently, and edit out any gadgetry that isn't earning its keep. I approach my kitchen the same way I do my closet: if an item hasn't been used in a year, it goes straight to the giveaway box.

A kitchen is an organic space, changing with the seasons and evolving with the family that it serves. I think the kitchen is the best place for family members to communicate their love for one another. Some of my most cherished memories involve my children helping me in the kitchen when they were little. Now they're accomplished cooks, and their own kids are following in their footsteps. This is how the kitchen brings people together.

PREVIOUS PAGE
On a high floor in midtown Manhattan, an existing multifunction kitchen was located in a niche just off the common room. We opened an eight-foot-wide slot in the wall between them. Sliding doors plastered to match the common room walls let the owners enjoy the amazing views from their wall of windows. For formal events, the doors can be shut to conceal the kitchen. A second entry door provides easy circulation for serving staff.

OPPOSITE
In the same kitchen, a counter-height chef's table is where friends sit when they drop by and where the owners dine when they are alone. Pillar candles on a steel chandelier provide soft, fluttering light for romantic dinners. A well-stocked bar behind a pivoting door also provides wine storage. To reinforce the feeling of sanctuary the walls of the kitchen were painted rich concrete gray to quiet the bright white carrara marble floors and countertops.

FOLLOWING PAGES
This kitchen is designed carefully to be a quiet element in a larger common area. It is dark and elegant but well lit. In feng shui, black is the color of water and therefore brings prosperity. A patch of red is included to stimulate the appetite. This is clearly not a kitchen for an avid cook. The fridge is more likely to contain Champagne and sparkling water than a pile of produce. The interior of the cabinets is lacquered in Chinese red to give a startling flash of unpredictable color.

KITCHEN ESSENTIALS

A BAR

If you can, open the kitchen to the common room, and separate the two spaces with a bar or island countertop, with seats to encourage lingering—or from which to coax assistants into the cooking fray. Use concrete, stone, or other heat-resistant materia,l as well as stainless steel for the counter.

VENTILATION

The best kitchens have powerful, vented exhaust systems and windows that open wide. If yours has neither, stick to less malodorous cooking at home. Downdraft and non-ducting systems can help cut down on oily smoke and clingy odors, but they're best for cooking techniques like poaching, steaming, and roasting, which produce less smoke than sautéing and pan searing.

LIGHTING

Use several light sources for separate areas of the kitchen and place them all on dimmer switches. This way, you can blast your prep area, sink, and stove with bright light while you're working, then dial it down to a warm glow when it's time to serve and people are circling hungrily by the counter. Think of the atmospheric glow of good restaurants.

HONESTY

Is your kitchen primarily for entertaining, experimenting, or serving takeout? The more honest you are about the way you use this room, the better its design will suit you. Just as a neglected professional-grade kitchen may be a source of stagnation, a dormitory kitchen will cramp the style of an avid cook. Make an honest assessment of your needs and then plan accordingly.

STORAGE

Arrange storage to keep the items you use daily close at hand. Coffee cups, for example, belong above the kettle or coffeemaker. Store dishes close to the dishwasher and knives near the chopping block. Install shallow shelves so that you can see jars or spices at a glance. Anything you use regularly belongs on a an easily accessible prime -real-estate shelf.

EQUIPMENT

A powerful, preferably gas range is a huge asset. A convection toaster oven or microwave is useful for heating everyday dishes. A capacious refrigerator encourages healthier eating habits by affording room for bulky fruits and vegetables. A small beverage fridge in the common room is a luxury. Use stove-to-table cookware, such as Le Creuset, to save energy.

TOOLS

Invest in three great knives—a paring, a chef's, and a serrated—and keep them sharp. A toolbar is ideal for storing cooking utensils you use most often—spatula, slotted spoon, strainer, whisk, and ladle. Hand tools like peelers and zesters must be deemed necessary; otherwise, show them the door. Keep an abundance of simple serving utensils and plates, rather than a tiny set of precious ones.

SURFACES

A kitchen, like a bathroom, should look clean but not clinical. If the kitchen is part of the common room, lay the same flooring throughout, whether that is bamboo, concrete, cork, or more traditional materials like wood or stone. Counters should be stain-resistant. Man-made products like manufactured stone work well for this; natural stones are porous and can be prone to staining.

STAGING AREAS

Keep a clear area for incoming groceries. You should not need a Sherpa guide to find food items in your kitchen. Allocate specific areas in your refrigerator and pantry for grains, meat, dairy, produce, or vegan protein, and then teach everyone in the household this system. As for garbage, allow at least four receptacles to handle paper, plastic bottles, metal recycling, and non-recyclables.

FACT-GATHERING BEFORE DESIGN

WHAT HAPPENS IN YOUR KITCHEN? This information is critical when designing a hardworking kitchen that truly supports the way you live. Yet our perceptions about what we do in the kitchen and how we eat can be wildly off base.

THE BEST WAY TO START is to identify the critical path of your project, noting all of the milestones you need to reach in order to complete it. At least one month before you begin designing this room, start a diary. The minute you feel the tiniest frisson of annoyance while you're in your current kitchen—even if you're not cooking—make a note of it in the diary. After two weeks, review your diary, and see what annoyances have been cropping up regularly. How you actually use your kitchen and the recurring problem zones will emerge, and you can figure out what changes are required to make operations simpler.

IT'S ALSO HELPFUL TO CREATE A DRAWING of every shelf and drawer and record what is in every single one. Be warned: you will not like this, but please force yourself to do it. It will provide enormous perspective, help you make wise decisions about your kitchen layout, and save you hours of future frustration in your current or newly designed kitchen. An enormous kitchen is seldom an efficient one. Whenever I see a restaurant kitchen, I'm amazed at the amount of deliciousness produced in so few square feet. For efficiency, the four main work zones—sink, range, refrigerator, and prep area—should be only two to five steps from one another. If there are two cooks in the house, plan for two bodies swirling around each other with wet, hot, and sharp objects, and go with the larger of these measurements.

OPPOSITE
A signature Clodagh detail, the interior of this custom-built cabinet is painted in the owner's favorite bright color. Every time the doors are opened a little jolt of excitement is released into the room. Narrow shelves are just the right size to hold glasses.

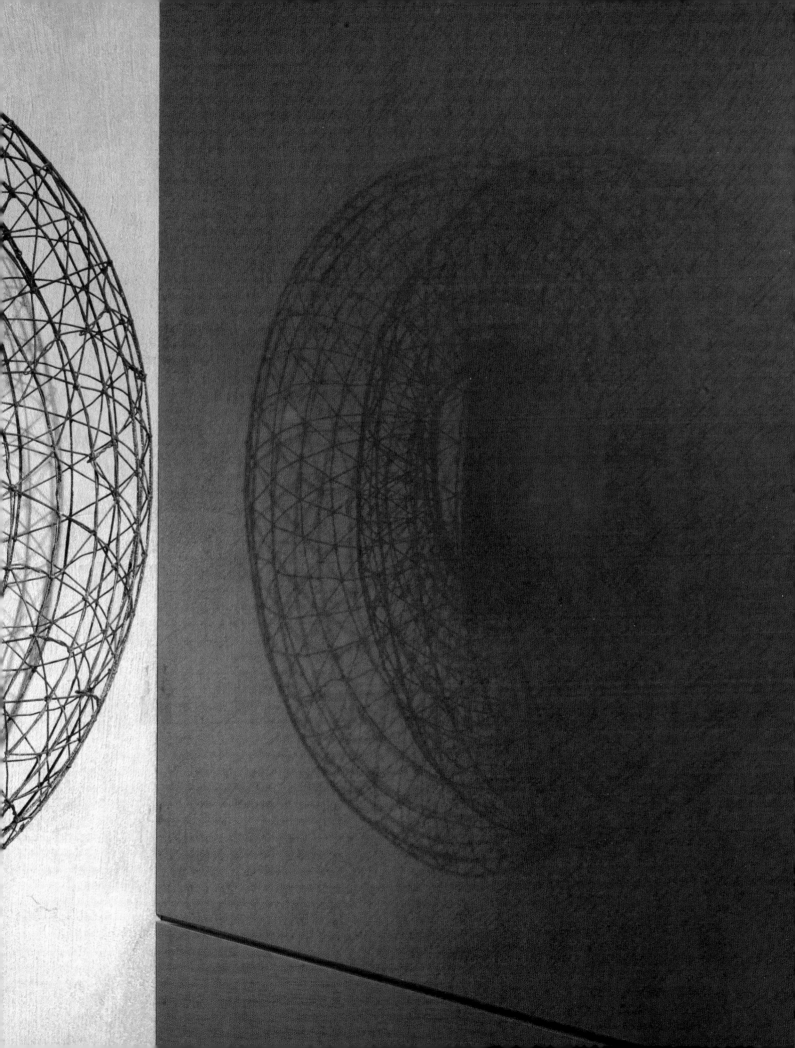

THE FIVE SENSES

Our senses anchor us in the present. They are important to home design because awareness of our physical senses makes us inhabit our homes more fully, which contributes to better design choices and reinforces an atmosphere of sanctuary. Good design appeals to all five of them—touch, sight, smell, sound, and taste—by placing things pleasurable to each throughout the rooms. This task is simplest in the kitchen, where all senses are most richly engaged. Touch: the soft fuzzy skin of a peach or the warm handle of a skillet. Sight: piles of colorful prepped vegetables waiting to be sautéed, or a loved one sampling sauce from a wooden spoon. Smell: the salivation-inducing fragrance of a pie working its way to the table, or wafts of pungent minced cilantro and preserved lemons. Sound: the pop of the cork reluctantly leaving a good bottle of wine, or the crash of ice cubes falling into the icemaker. Taste: the flavor a favorite spice on the tip of your tongue, or the taste of sweet orange juice in the back of your mouth. To these five senses I like to add a sixth, the sense of time: reflective elements that celebrate the movement of light and the changing of seasons, and organic surfaces like wood that patina gracefully to show the passage of years, are important in any kitchen.

PREVIOUS PAGES
The color red is a fantastic stimulant for the appetite. An Asian eel-fishing basket is wired with a halogen bulb to cast light and shadows on the wall. Tools and implements that were used for another purpose are good things to use around your sanctuary as they hold the energy of the hands that worked with them.

OPPOSITE
Foods to encourage healthy snacking are kept out in the open in clear glass jars, rather than stashed away in a cupboard. Similarly, fresh herbs are container-grown in plain view on the counter, where leaves and sprigs can be snipped and added to the simmering pot. An island provides ample storage for pots and pans on its working side, as well as drawers for table-cloths, napkins, and other entertainment supplies on the side facing the adjacent common area.

FOLLOWING PAGES
In this kitchen a satiny, graphite-colored sealed concrete slab is edged with lac-quered raw steel. On the cook's side, open drawers are loaded with handsome cook-ware. Spices and hand-tools are stored in closed drawers on either side of the cooktop. A slot above the stove provides excellent ventilation. A reclaimed-wood floor runs through both the common room and kitchen to unify the two areas.

The bedroom is the most private room in the home—both literally and figuratively. In the literal sense, it is separate from the kitchen, the family room, and other bustling public spaces. Figuratively, it is where our most private selves can emerge. Consider what goes on (and comes off) in the bedroom: sleep, that most solitary and vulnerable of acts; sex, which for many is the epitome of intimacy and exposure. Here daydreaming, which bedrooms are perfect for, transports us to a fragile, inward-looking place.

RESTING, DREAMING, SEX

Because the bedroom is where we let our guard down, it's essential to get the planning just right, starting with the bed. It amazes me that although we spend a third of our lives sleeping, people often choose their bed like they would an item off a fast-food menu. Please, please do not buy a mattress online. It is critical to test out different models in the showroom until you find the mattress that is a perfect fit for your body. If you're prone to back pain or sleepless nights, this one decision could make the difference. What goes on the mattress is important, too. A combination of soft and firm pillows for sleeping and reading is key, as are silky soft sheets and hypo-allergenic blankets and slipcovers.

Once the bed is in place, turn your attention to what's happening around it. Remember that only a handful of activities should take place in the bedroom: sleeping, reading, conversation, relaxing, and sex. This means no work papers piled on the bedside table or laptops on the pillows. I don't think a television belongs in the bedroom, but if you must, consider investing in one that can be hidden from sight behind a panel or screen.

Strategic manipulation of the elements is another crucial aspect of bedroom design; for example, while the afternoon sun slanting through a window can be a blissful sight, come bedtime many people need the total darkness afforded by blackout blinds. Similarly, the ability to adjust the room temperature with a ceiling fan or air conditioner can be as effective as a lullaby at inducing slumber.

The secret to bedroom design is tailoring this very private space to your equally personal needs. Do this correctly, and the result will be a retreat within the already safe confines of your home—a sanctuary like no other.

PREVIOUS PAGE
A naturally edged slice of a massive tree, polished to satiny glow, is the headboard. A minimal reading light provides a tiny metal element to balance the others in the room. Bed linens are sexy, low maintenance, and luxurious.

OPPOSITE
A platform bed the color of dark chocolate is piled with creamy textured bed linens from Donna Karan Home and a selection of firm and soft pillows. The wide platform visually connects the bed and the headboard.

OPPOSITE
A warm clay-colored plaster key wall houses a horizontal fireplace bisecting an art ledge. Two comfortable swivel chairs invite intimate conversation, or quiet meditation overlooking trees. The bed is positioned against a solid wall and the ceiling slants away from it, up to a view of treetops. The colors of the room are grounding and sensual.

FOLLOWING PAGES
Silent white plaster bounces uniform light in this quiet room. Steel-flanked walls lead to a bathroom luminous with frosted glass and café-au-lait-colored concrete. A stretch of cushioned window seat and a rug of loopy vanilla tendrils texture the quiet space. Outside of the frame of this photograph, a scented *ylang ylang* candle engages the sense of smell.

BEDROOM ESSENTIALS

SEATING

In terms of furniture, all you really need in a bedroom is a comfortable bed and solid bedside tables with a drawer. But if space allows, a chair, ottoman, and a small table are supportive supplemental furnishings. A window seat is also lovely, and a pair of dedicated trays for your bedroom may prompt a partner to bring you the perfect cup of tea.

BEAUTY

From the vantage point of the bed, your eyes should rest on something beautiful. A view to the outdoors is ideal, but art works as well. The role of paintings, sculpture, or photography in a bedroom is to bring peace, a smile, joy, and sensual pleasure when you rest your eyes on the object before or after sleep.

LUXURY

Your bedroom should impart quiet luxury—to your bare skin, to your delicate sense of smell, and to your tired eyes. A cashmere or cotton-cashmere blanket delivers classic comfort. Soft terry cloth robes or silk kimonos bring another layer of luxury to the room. In addition, a signature scent can be erotic or calming; you can mix your own if you purchase a diffuser.

THE BED AND PILLOWS

Get a king-size bed if space permits. Meet your partner in the middle for fun, and stay on either side for rest. Your mattress and pillows should be hypo-allergenic and firm. If one of you weighs a lot more than the other, buy two inner springs geared to your individual weights and one big mattress pad to go over the top.

LIGHT AND DARK

Control the lighting environment in the bedroom: install bedside reading lights; a very dim "love light" to make you look fantastic; and a large, bright light for cleaning. Put all the fixtures on dimmer switches, so that you can easily adjust the atmosphere. Have both blackout shades and sheer shades for the windows—one for creating darkness, the other for privacy.

THE ELEMENTS

It is good feng shui to represent all five elements in the bedroom. Wood is good for the bed frame. Stone floors bring in the earth element. A candle provides the fire element. There should be very little metal in the bedroom—a metal reading lamp is plenty. Water can be represented by a photograph or painting of the ocean or by a small tabletop fountain.

QUIET AND SOUND

Make sure to include equipment to play music, sleep-inducing soundtracks, or white noise in the bedroom. In addition to being pleasurable, these work to muffle sound. If you are building a new bedroom, insulate the walls. Layered fabrics and textured materials also provide natural sound absorption and reduce unwanted echoes.

STORAGE

Anything stored in a bedroom should be kept organized and in good repair. Disorder is a source of mental static that is not conducive to either rest or sex. Under the bed, store only the items pertaining to the bed such as linens and spare pillows. If you have the option, separate the closet from the bed with a half-wall, settee, or large ottoman.

PRIVACY

Doors with locks on them and good window coverings are a must for making you feel secure when you sleep or spend time alone with your partner. Address ways to dampen sound. Always have a lockable drawer to keep items you don't want your children, cleaning help, or mother to see.

THREE COMMON MISTAKES
TO AVOID

CROWDING: Both photographs of people and television sets invite an unrestful state of mind. They are akin to having a crowd in the room while you sleep. If you insist on having a TV, make sure you can turn it off from the bed, or better yet hide it away before going to sleep. Photos are best if you can't see them from bed. And make sure that you have earphones for the person who wants to watch TV in bed, and an eye mask for the one who does not.

VISIBLE PAPERWORK: Make sure you can't see any paperwork from your bed. If your home office must be part of your bedroom, it should not be visible from your bed; otherwise, these papers will infiltrate your thoughts while you sleep. Slide a panel over the unpaid bills and unanswered mail on the desk.

BOOKCASES WITHOUT DOORS: Books are as demanding as papers from the office—their titles beckon and seduce. Add doors or shades to existing bookshelves to bring a look of uniformity to the books. If you like to read in bed, bring the book you are reading to the bedroom, or have a bedside book of daily quotes or a new magazine that you rotate in and out.

OPPOSITE
In the corner of a tiny studio apartment, a built-in queen-size bed doubles as a lounging sofa. It is dressed with textured opulent silks and a coffee-color spread. The accent pillows are violet, the color of the crown *chakra*, and support dreaming. A feathered African headdress splashes more color and absorbs some sound. Drawers set under the mattress store spare linens and towels.

FOLLOWING PAGES
In a master bedroom, a high-backed window seat equipped with good reading lights invites a relaxed face-to-face chat, a double date with two good books, or a quick nap (sometimes all three in succession). Deep drawers set below provide valuable storage space for out-of-season linens. The privacy shades let in light but blur the view into the room from outside.

SLEEPING WELL

Sleep expert Dr. Rubin Naiman recommends these five essential steps to good sleep:

Control light and darkness: for dusk, use dimmer switches to lower light levels, moon eyeglasses, or motion-detector night-lights. For evening, lower black blinds and tape over LEDs on phones or alarms. For dawn, use built-in sunrise simulation systems or drape-draw timers. Simulate night sounds: A built-in speaker system with nature sounds or white noise is great for inducing sleep. Noise-abating windowpanes, drapes, and insulation can block out unwanted noise from outside. Create a sleep-supportive atmosphere: install high-efficiency (HEPA) filtration, EMF/subtle energy field management, CO_2 detectors, an aromatherapy system, and a local thermostat for circadian rhythm temperature control. Provide optimal bed and bedding: emphasize organic, hypo-allergenic, and natural fibers and materials. Minimize off gassing by using natural products that are also fire-retardant and mite-resistant. Design for sleep: Proper bed placement for your space is essential. In addition, use deep, warm colors for both bedding and wall paint.

Besides taking care of your sleep needs, treat your guests to a good night's sleep. Provide sleep masks, books of amusing quotes for the bedside, reading lights, and comfortable robes. Supply a bottle of water, towels, and a set of pillows—one firm, one soft—for each guest. Welcome overnight visitors with a bud vase or a small bowl of seasonal fruit, and a cozy blanket to keep the chill off. The bathroom should contain well-organized toiletries, including new toothbrushes. Leave a set of travel-size amenities in the bathroom, including standard pain and headache remedies. Providing hanging space and shelf space for clothing will make guests feel welcome, even if the room they're sleeping in is normally your home office. Remember, think boutique hotel for guest rooms.

OPPOSITE
An art light sprays shadows on the deep taupe walls of this quiet, comforting co-ed guest bedroom. The side table is stocked with a small kit of toiletries, nuts, chocolate, and a bottle of water.

SERENITY AND STORAGE

The key to maintaining a serene bedroom is to remove every opportunity for clutter and stagnation. If you have space, separate your closet from your bedroom. A closet in the bedroom calls for a great deal of self-control to keep it organized and clean. Plus, with a closet nearby, the bed becomes a landing place for clothing rather than a sanctuary for your tired, or sexy, body. If you have a closet in your bedroom, like most of us, clean it regularly so it is not bursting at the seams.

Avoid conflict: do not share your closet. If one person is a neatnik and the other a collector, closet conflict is bound to break out. However, if you must share, draw a clear line between your space and your partner's, and bring in third-party arbitration to make sure a fair balance is set. Some people are folders and others are hangers. If you fold, limit stacks to two or three folded garments; otherwise, the stacks will tumble every time you try to pull something out. Use matching hangers, some with clips for pants and skirts and some with pads for delicate sweaters.

Work with a closet company to maximize and organize the space. A custom closet preserves your wardrobe (and your sanity), and it's a fantastic investment. Before the company comes to measure, make sure you do a brutal wardrobe edit. Send bags of retired outfits to your nearest charity, so that you are not paying to store clothing that is past its shelf life.

OPPOSITE
A crushed-copper-mesh hanging lamp glows against a corrugated, burnished *papier-mâché* wall in this tactile, textured master bedroom. The rug is splashed with light-catching silk. The lights seeping from the shelf and up the wall are the feng shui equivalent of fire, and fuel passions.

FOLLOWING PAGES
For the creation of healing design, the selection of linens and the products with which you wash them is vital to well-being. Luxury lies in touch, and bed linens touch more of your naked skin than any other element in the home. In this bedroom, textured organic bed linens are patterned with eucalyptus shadows and stitched with dressmaker details.

A child's room is the backdrop against which he or she conducts the astonishing work of growing to maturity. Because children are so very present and adaptable, they may need a sanctuary even more than adults. The role of a child's room is to foster his or her emerging spirit and humor, rather than indulge an ever-changing idea of a dream bedroom. Cartooned walls and beds in the shape of a glass slipper or race car don't stir a child's imagination, but force it into a corner. I'm not suggesting that you create a sterile, hospital-like environment; simplicity is not self-denial.

PLAYING, SLEEPING, DISCOVERING, CRYING, LAUGHING

A setting with rich, natural colors and simple furnishings will give your children's minds room to explore while making them comfortable in their own skins. Let your children share in the creation of their sanctuaries. They'll respect it more if they feel involved in the process, plus planning a space provides much from which to learn. The habits you teach your children stay with them. Something as simple as a peg on a wall will allow your kids to hang up their belongings and instill a healthy sense of ownership. Storage boxes labeled with each child's name will encourage similar responsibilities. And a giveaway box for those toys your children no longer use will give them an understanding of charity.

Children's needs change as they grow, so the design of their rooms must be flexible. This is why a neutral color scheme makes sense. Allow them to help choose their own bedspread and throw pillows. Ask them to select a paint color for the interior of their closet. Painting one section of wall with chalkboard paint, or hanging a roll of craft paper for drawing, allows your child's favorite colors to be expressed. The goal is not to impose your own tastes and sensibilities on your children, but rather to create an environment where they'll be free to discover their own.

PREVIOUS PAGE
Light-catching resin shelves provide flexible storage for books and toys in this Tribeca loft. This bright, open storage is suitable for children of any age; it is regularly purged to keep it up-to-date so that it does not stagnate. The books on the lowest shelf are easy to reach.

OPPOSITE
Pistachio green anchors the soothing palette chosen for this little girl's room. This restful hue symbolizes growth and harmony, so it's ideal for a child's space. Established in the geometric chest of drawers, it continues to the graphic, multi-toned artwork mounted to the wall. Because the child's bed is positioned on the opposite wall, the lively painting is the first thing she sees in the morning, which is good feng shui.

FOLLOWING PAGES
A glamorous girl's room sports her favorite colors: pistachio and blue. The translucent resin shelves are stacked with her current favorites. A cuddly area rug softens the room and absorbs sound. The bed is placed against a wall in a perfect feng shui position. Mother and daughter chose the linens to play with the lovely tones in the room, and these can be changed easily.

KID'S ROOM ESSENTIALS

RITUALS AND HABITS

Children learn through ritual. Habits help them place themselves in the world. A full-length mirror in a child's room or bathroom will provoke just enough self-awareness to make him or her mindful of grooming and posture. Designating an area where children can place toys or clothing for donation will teach them to be giving. A warm lavender-scented bath and cuddle is a great presleep ritual.

FLEXIBILITY

Planning a child's room requires much foresight. A baby will interact with this space differently from a toddler and a teen. And a second child may come and share the room. Obviously, you can't balance all those needs at once. But you can establish patterns; for example, dedicate the room to sleep and play as opposed to homework.

STORAGE

Your child's room should be equipped with adequate storage, in the form of bins, boxes, and a bureau or built-in drawers. Make sure the storage is accessible, both to you and to your child. Label containers by name and consider a color-coded system for preschoolers. Bookshelves are a natural for children's rooms, but purge them often so they stay current.

FURNITURE

A generous armchair or a comfy rocker is where you'll nurse, cuddle, and read stories. When the child is old enough to leave the crib, I like to put in a queen-size unit or a twin bed with a trundle underneath that can be pulled out for sleepovers. Supply enough drawer and closet space to make it easy for children to put away their possessions.

CREATIVITY

When a child is young, nurture the extraordinary spirit and creativity that hasn't yet been curtailed by school and peer criticism. Leave walls neutral, avoiding cutesy patterns. Stock the room with chalkboards, drawing pads, and easels; the more canvases on which to create, the better. If the child dreams of a character, let her express herself on one of these areas.

FLOORING

A child's play area calls for soft flooring, but wall-to-wall carpet provides a vector for dust mites and germs. Instead, opt for an organic, easy-to-clean material such as linoleum. It cleans with a damp mop and it's made of natural materials. If you like the look of hardwood, bamboo is a sustainable option. Its boards can be covered with a soft area rug that's easy to lift up and clean.

SLEEPING

Restorative sleep is so important to maintaining a child's balance and equilibrium. Blackout shades are great for establishing healthy sleep patterns. A cozy bed with cotton sheets and bedspreads anchors any bedroom. And a sound system on which to play classical music or recordings of nature is an essential sleep aide for tots. Older children will appreciate this too.

GROWING PLANTS

Live plants and flowers make a child's room more beautiful, while at the same time reinforcing his or her connection to the natural world. Smelling flowers or caressing plant leaves, will give children an affinity for certain scents and textures that later in life will serve as instant triggers for childhood memories.

SAFETY

Be sensible and compromise: don't make the room a repository for sharp objects, but at the same time don't pad the walls and move electric outlets to the ceiling. Find the middle ground; for example, tethering bookshelves to walls, using safe outlet guards, and eliminating cord blind pulls. Consult a reliable parenting Website for up-to-date information.

OPPOSITE

This baby's room incorporates both open and closed storage. Toys are stored out of sight and brought out a few at a time, so they stay interesting. Whites are some of my favorite paint shades for children's rooms, as they are clean, bright, and not overbearing. The inside of these cabinets can be painted one or more rich, surprising colors as soon as the child is old enough to select them. The TV is used as an educational tool.

THREE WAYS TO MAKE A CHILD'S ROOM CALMER

THEMED DECOR: Avoid over-decorating the room with themed commercial images. Instead, allow children to create their own motifs. Installing chalkboard and corkboard surfaces throughout the space will encourage your little ones to maintain revolving displays of their own artwork. There are even chalkboard paints that make it possible to turn an entire wall, or just the back of a closet door, into an erasable tablet.

CONTROL TV AND COMPUTERS: These electronics are essential learning tools in today's world, so it's not always advisable to ban them from children's bedrooms. But it's important to control how they're seen and used. Flat-screen televisions and computer monitors can be concealed behind movable screens. Parents can lock out channels that aren't appropriate for young viewers. If there is a desk with a computer, have a sliding screen or other movable wall to give your child a break from it. However, to keep children from retreating too often into their bedrooms, it's best for homework to be done in a common area.

CONCENTRATED PLAYING: A child's room should not be the only play area in the home, or the child who uses it may have a hard time relaxing there. Consider incorporating play into the common room to encourage spending time together. Create a TV/play/game area where the whole family can have fun. I also believe that outdoor forts and play zones are irresistible.

OPPOSITE
A boy's room provides all the elements he needs for sleep, reading, and homework. The inside of his closet is painted a strong blue as blue is a calming color for bedrooms. Orange, a good color for communication, is picked out in accessories.

A SHELF OF ONE'S OWN

While the whole house should not become a playground, I encourage you to incorporate children's areas or items geared specifically toward them within other rooms. After all, it is their house as much as it is yours. Here are some ideas:

- Create a tough, washable studio area where they can make things with clay and paint and paper.

- Include a seat they can reach in the living room.

- Provide a low bar or peg where they can hang their own coats.

- Install a towel hook they can reach in the bathroom.

- Have a designated shelf or cubbyhole for their toys and toiletries.

- Add a sliding step in the bottom of the sink vanity, where they can stand to wash up and groom themselves.

- Create a window box where your kids can grow flowers or herbs.

- Designate a patch in the garden for children to take care of plants.

OPPOSITE
The simplicity of this limestone-paved bathroom allows a small girl to add a gossamer pink light. The bottom drawer is actually a step that allows her to reach the sink on her own. Later on when she is bigger, the step flips over to become a drawer again.

GREEN PLANNING

Nowhere are healthy, sustainable building practices more important than in a child's room. Young people are even more susceptible than adults to dangerous products and materials; for example, those containing lead paint or formaldehyde. Fortunately, there are many resources aimed at helping homeowners make healthy, eco-friendly decisions. Leadership in Energy and Environmental Design (LEED) offers guidelines and rating systems for sustainable products and practices. (Refer to the U.S. Green Building Council's *Green Home Guide* at www.greenhomeguide.org).

If you're decorating a child's room, be sure to choose paints that are low in VOCs—short for volatile organic compounds. These solvents are released into the air and can be harmful when breathed. The VOC content will be indicated on the paint can label; fewer than fifty VOCs per gallon is considered low. Choose sustainable materials that are easy on Mother Earth, as well as the workers who produce them; for example, I frequently use reclaimed-timber flooring, rather than wood that has to be cut from present-day forests. Bamboo is another sustainable flooring option; it's a fast-growing woody grass that doesn't have to be cut down completely to harvest.

Green practices should continue after the child's room is complete. Use only nontoxic cleaning products; you'll be amazed at the cleaning power of items like lemon, vinegar, and baking powder. And be mindful of the toys you bring into the space, choosing ones that are made of natural, lead-free materials. Last but not least, pass sustainable habits on to your children by encouraging them to donate toys they no longer use.

OPPOSITE
A child's room is about sleep and play, so an assortment of bright, soft toys with engaging expressions are just the thing to take down for a cuddle before climbing under the covers. Objects with different textures—some furry, some smooth, some hard—will stimulate a child's sense of touch. A collection of favorite books should be handy for sleep-inducing bedtime stories.

FOLLOWING PAGES
Vibrant colors animate this child's room, which is organized around discrete play stations. The curtained corner serves multiple functions. When the child is feeling theatrical, it serves as a stage for impromptu performances. When his mood is introspective, it offers a hiding place where he can find alone time. Every surface in the room can be wiped clean easily, keeping germs at bay.

Our bodies are roughly 70 percent water. No wonder we love to bathe, as we acknowledge and commune with our most important element. We spend as many as seven hours a week in the bathroom—cleansing, shaving, applying makeup, lounging in a scented tub, listening to music in the shower, ridding our bodies of toxins. For about two of those hours we're naked, and nakedness means vulnerability, so this room has to be conceived in very particular ways.

GROOMING, CLEANING, CLEANSING

Indeed, the bathroom, along with the kitchen, is one of two main centers of wellness in the home. Unfortunately, people don't always see this room as one to be lived in. It may be that, unlike kitchens, bathrooms are not public spaces, on display to convey your tastes for every visitor. But this is precisely why they demand such careful attention. The bathroom is where you start and end each day (with a few visits in between).

Start the design process by making a list of what the space means to you. A bathroom is about the creation of life-enhancing rituals that will be observed and enjoyed on a daily basis. If sinking into a hot tub is how you like to unwind, make sure there's plenty of room for a soaking tub. Or you may wish to make space for a double shower, so that you and your partner can experience the pleasures of water together. If you practice herbalism, grow a favorite aromatic healing herb in a small window box. I even like to keep a tiny refrigerator in my bathroom, stocked with chocolates and Champagne.

Of course, there are practical concerns as well. Above all, every item in a bathroom must have its place. This will keep surfaces clear and cut down on the visual clutter that is anathema to peace and recovery. Because space is usually limited, every inch counts in a bathroom (it's like a boat in that sense), so it's important to implement vertical storage devices, such as towel bars and medicine cabinets.

By marrying the sensible with the sensual, you'll create a bathroom that offers a true sanctuary experience, just as a spa offers an escape from the stressful public world into one of privacy, quiet, and calm.

PREVIOUS PAGE
The walls of this skylit home spa are clad with calming slate gray tiles. The water in this Sok™ tub is effervescent with small bubbles. Water flows over the edges into an outer basin. There is a built-in chromatherapy feature that illuminates the water in any *chakra* color to revive your energy. Shower and toilet are tucked behind separate glass doors. The tub is placed directly under the skylight to afford some sky gazing while soaking.

OPPOSITE
A play of translucence and opacity textures this airy bath. A boulder, neatly sliced in two and set in the concrete floor, serves as a seating bench and neatly grasps a sheet of nonreflective glass. Three sides of this shower are sandblasted for privacy.

FOLLOWING PAGES
Left: A long, cantilevered cast-concrete trough sink sits quietly under three massive mirrored medicine cabinets. It is easy to share space in this bathroom. A custom teak tray in the center holds amenities and towels. Rather than on a bar, towels drape naturally on slim hooks. Concrete is easy to maintain and warmer underfoot or to the hand than porcelain. Right: The solid warmth of a teak bath mat set over the concealed drain is welcoming to bare feet. To the right is the section of boulder.

OPPOSITE

Left: The layers and transparencies in this guest bath defy its compact size. The walls are tiled with corten-colored ceramic rectangles. Sliding frosted doors and a teak shower mat (stepping onto wood when your feet are wet is a tactile pleasure) lends privacy, light, and strength to the space. Right: A burnished cast-aluminum sink sits on steel rods in this efficient guest bathroom. Amber plaster over bronze metal mesh textures the walls of the forced perspective alcove. Amber is a reinforcing color that provides a moment of peace and warmth for a simple hand cleanse.

FOLLOWING PAGES

Left: A combination of natural and artificial light bathes a his-and-hers vanity in abundant illumination. Mirror-mounted faucets limit clutter on the countertop. Right, clockwise from top left: The ridges in these cast-concrete tiles provide visual texture and dampen sound. A cast countertop swoops into an integrated sink, leaving a smooth stretch to harbor amenities. The entire bathroom is lined with reclaimed-wood paneling, which also forms the door to a concealed toilet. The bold door pull of cast bronze adds texture and bling to the space. Three aromatherapy candles sit on a chunky wood built-in ledge lined with steel.

BATHROOM ESSENTIALS

MIRRORS

Mirrors are more important in the bathroom than in any other room of the house. Not only are they helpful for grooming, they visually expand this often compact space. Mirrored cabinets have the added bonus of a storage space. A magnifying mirror with an integrated light is a must for makeup application or shaving. Three-way mirrors let you see the back of your head.

THE TOILET

A bathroom is about elimination as much as cleansing. Ideally, there will be room to cordon off a separate area to house the toilet. This can be done in an alcove, with a half wall, or even with a screen. Choose a low-flow model that conserves water; save water by selecting a toilet with two-button flushes—one for liquid and one for solids.

THE BATH AND SHOWER

Water takes many forms in the bathroom. A shower can massage your body vigorously. Luxury shower panels with multiple jets and multicolored chromatherapy lights are attractive options. Tubs can be as still as a reflecting pool or roiling with bubbles. Visit bath showrooms, peruse design magazines, and think back on the best bathing experiences from your travels.

TEMPERATURE

Naked bodies like to be warm. A heated towel rack is a true luxury in any bathroom, allowing you to wrap yourself in warmth after a shower or bath. Your feet will tingle against the warm embrace of a tile floor pulsing with radiant heat. An exhaust fan is essential for eliminating moisture and maintaining a comfortable temperature.

SHARING

Make the main part of the bathroom a social center. Long, deep soaking tubs are superb for any relationship. The bathroom is where you create and enjoy the gentle rituals of cleansing your body and your mind. Install a double shower so you can do this together. Sharing needn't only be romantic: a large whirlpool tub allows the whole family to unite.

STORAGE

Shallow, wall-mounted cabinets work well for medicines and grooming supplies. Assign each family member a shelf for personal items. Reserve deep cabinets for towels, and save the space beneath the vanity for cleaning products. If you are in construction, build a floor-to-ceiling cabinet into the wall between the studs to hold toilet paper, soap, and toothpaste.

LIGHTING

You need two kinds of light in the bathroom: one for getting ready and one for winding down. Natural morning light streaming into the bathroom is extremely upbeat. Many mirrors have a built-in fluorescent or LED light so that you can see what's going on with your makeup or shaving. When you're relaxing, dim lights low, ignite a fragrant candle, and lounge in a hot tub.

MAINTENANCE

To minimize upkeep, choose surfaces that are easy to wipe clean. Floors and walls tiled in stone or ceramic are a cinch to maintain. Painted walls are also easy, provided you opt for a semigloss finish. Keep toiletries from cluttering up the vanity: not only do they look messy, but they attract dust. Stock natural cleaning products for your body and for your bathroom.

MATERIALS

Surfaces that are calm, comfortable, and understated work well in a bathroom. Stainless steel is cool and easy to clean. Copper is warm and glowing. Slate, tile, and frosted glass are also good options. I like a combination of man-made and natural materials; for example, metal walls and a stone floor.

INSPIRATION

INSTALL A FIREPLACE: This is the ultimate indulgence in any bathroom. Lounge in a hot bath and watch the flames dance, and then perch on the hearth to dry your hair. There are many beautiful, compact gas-burning fireplaces on the market that can be installed easily in a bathroom. The beauty of gas is it turns on and off with the flick of a switch, and there's no wood to haul in and out.

PLAN FOR SOUND: After your tub is full, the sound of trickling water will fill the air of your peaceful bathroom. Alternatively, you can open a window to hear the world outside while you are relaxing; even city noise sounds wonderfully remote from the safe sanctuary of your bathroom. A small radio, CD player, or speakers from your central sound system can bring in Chopin or rap music.

ADD A CHAISE: This is one of the simplest pleasures, if you have space. There's a reason why they put chaises in spas. A catnap after grooming and bathing when you are squeaky clean and destressed is the height of relaxation. And, tuck a refrigerator into an underused corner of the bathroom, or in the base of a storage column. Use yours to store special treats.

OPPOSITE
A natural wood storage column contains everything a tiny bathroom needs, including a tiny refrigerator stocked with water. The translucent door breathes light into the room. The same pale concrete gray plaster is used throughout, even in the shower, creating a seamless serene space. The concrete floor matches the color of the walls. Its radiant heat comforts the owners' cold morning feet.

FOUR INDULGENCES

DESIGN A POWDER ROOM: Pull out the stops for these tiny nooks. Use one of your favorite colors in saturated tones, and feel free to be as playful or as dramatic as you wish. A cacophony of patterns in a powder room may leave your guests reeling, but the bottom line is that this room is only a moment of fun, unlike the regularly experienced master bath.

TRAVEL: Keep extra toiletries lined up so that they'll be there when you need them. This makes it easy to accept a last-minute invitation and hop on a flight with minimal preparation. Keep travel kits for each member of your family. Stock them with miniatures of your favorite products in a transparent plastic bag so that there are no problems with airport security. Have a separate bag for prescription drugs and vitamins. Include hidden delights to bring comfort along the way, such as a cold mask for jet-lagged eyes that can be activated once you reach your destination.

OUTDOOR BATHING: An outdoor shower is one of life's great pleasures, if you have the space to install it. I love them even when it's raining or cold. Place a chaise nearby for sun drying in warm weather. Look for one made of weather-resistant materials, such as teak; any cushions should be covered in waterproof fabric. A whirlpool is a delightful way to unwind and watch the stars, in warm and cold climates alike. Best of all, you don't have to worry about splashing too much.

BOTANICALS: If you don't have the space for these outdoor options, give indoor bathrooms a sense of the outdoors by planting an aromatherapy garden near a window. I still remember from my childhood the scent of wet lilacs drifting through an open casement window in the bathroom.

OPPOSITE
A sink carved out of a piece of natural stone sits on a concrete-topped vanity in this powder room. The floor is tiled with smooth pebbles. Since this is a shoes-off home, guests get a moment of reflexology as they wash their hands; violet is the owners' favorite color and stimulates the *sahasrara*, or crown *chakra*, which supports passion and understanding.

A home spa in a townhouse is the perfect place for a lazy, self-renewing afternoon for one or two. The room shares a fireplace with the open dressing room. A bronze and blue iridescent microfiber drape closes to leave the person soaking in the tub to his or her private musings. The concealed shower has a tree and rooftop view—a toilet is tucked away behind a glass door.

FOLLOWING PAGES

Left: A satin white porcelain sink with a rear overflow drain sits on a blonde slab of limestone. The custom vanity was inspired by kitchen cabinetry. It includes two narrow cabinets that use full-extension hardware to slide out and reveal pantrylike shelves that are perfect for small toiletries. Hidden compartments in bathroom vanities are also good for concealing the kitty litter box. Right: In a small powder room, a travertine-colored concrete inverted cone sink is silhouetted against cast-concrete ziggurat tiles. "Large in small" is a mantra in our studio. Otherwise scaling everything to fit makes a small room look like a dollhouse.

OPPOSITE
A lean, white Corian™ trough sink sits on a quartzite counter. Stainless steel faucets have textured detail that brings the warmth shared by all hand-tooled objects. Double faucets speed the morning routine for this working couple. A three-way medicine cabinet and a deep vanity provide shared storage, a cabinet each for the owners, and a way to check the back of their hair before they leave. The toilet is tucked behind a half wall.

FOLLOWING PAGES
An astounding, ever-changing view graces this cleft-stone-clad home spa over the water. A built-in bench slides through the glass wall of a huge steam shower and invites socializing. A thirteen-foot-wide graphite gray cast-concrete sink is the definition of generosity. Outside of the frame, floor-to-ceiling cabinets store towels and body care products. A toilet is tucked away behind electric glass that becomes opaque or transparent with the flip of a switch.

In my world, work equals passion. It exercises the mind and nourishes the soul. Whether you are writing, taking care of household business, studying, or doing tasks for your job, the place in your home dedicated to labor should quietly support you and your work. Work is solitary—not lonely, mind you. Group meetings may be required occasionally, but for the most part it is you and the computer screen or the sketch pad or whatever it is you use to record your thoughts and ideas.

WORKING, CREATING, COMMUNICATING

The first step toward creating a positive workspace is to establish boundaries. Interruption is the killer of creativity. Not everyone has the luxury of a separate room with a door for the workspace, but even in shared quarters it's usually possible to cordon off an area with a folding screen or other implied wall. If not, simply slipping on earphones may be enough to help you enter a private zone.

Once you've established this space, look for ways to tailor it to your physical and emotional needs. This includes not only bringing in a comfortable chair, but also things like placing an inspirational object in a special spot, or making a memory wall. My own home desk is an eleven-foot stretch of four-inch-thick white concrete, where I can spread plans or images or simply strip it and allow it to reflect light into the room when I am doing yoga. The desk's massive width helps to open my mind to inspiration. Strive for harmony on and around your desk by eliminating materials and supplies you don't need or use. Chances are you can survive with one or two favorite writing utensils, rather than a messy jarful. If an online dictionary is enough for you, why not donate your hard copy to a local school or library?

I'm truly enamored of wireless technology: is there anything more symbolically constrictive than a tangle of electric cords? A mirror over the desk, meanwhile, is a positive metaphor for reflection and important to good feng shui if your back is facing the room—it helps the flow of *chi* and is said to bring good fortune. Create serenity in this space, and it will stimulate the deep, meditative concentration required of true work. And your workroom will become one more refuge in your home sanctuary.

PREVIOUS PAGE
This space is pared down to the essentials: a simple, long desk with tiny lenticular mirrors cast into the concrete, and a white scoop of a chair. Everything else is storage and view. Printer and other wireless paraphernalia are hidden but waiting to serve behind steel-clad doors and drawers.

OPPOSITE
A bit of disciplined filing goes a long way in this workspace. The binders keep papers organized and look neutral and encouraging. A trip to a store devoted to storage and containers takes care of most storage woes. The papers in this room are filed daily, and reviewed and cleansed quarterly.

FOLLOWING PAGES
A concrete-topped desk for an art curator rests on a base made of one powerful slice of ½-inch steel. The concrete used here makes a warmer desktop than stone and its light catching qualities give depth and interest to the surface. Behind the desk, serried rows of binders hold artist portfolios.

WORKSPACE ESSENTIALS

PRIVACY

Daydreaming is a necessary part of creation, so it is great to have a workspace with inspiring views to the outdoors. A personal computer, whether in the form of a desktop or laptop, is a must-have for any home office, especially in the Internet age we live. Don't compromise your privacy by telling others your password.

WIRE MANAGEMENT

Go wireless with everything you can. Keyboards, mice, modems, and printers are all readily available in wireless form; just make sure to check their compatibility with your system. Keep any necessary cords in place with Velcro bands or, for a more permanent solution, try corralling wires with a grommet and chase. Whatever system you choose, always label wires.

SURFACE

A built-in surface implies permanence and establishes the right energy in a workspace. A sweep of plain concrete, a warm wood veneer, or even a satiny spread of stainless steel, are all excellent choices. Don't be hasty in your choice of material: touch it with your hands, and experience it with your eyes, before you settle on a final choice.

MEETING PLACE

If you hold meetings in your workspace, plan for sufficient seating; for example, keep additional folding chairs in a nearby closet. You'll send the wrong signal if your guests are uncomfortable. If necessary, relocate the meeting to a larger room. And if the workspace is a good distance from the kitchen, keep a small refrigerator stocked with beverages for your guests.

CAMOUFLAGE

If your workspace is not a dedicated room, put it out of sight when you are not working. Otherwise it will call to you constantly, and make it hard to relax and enjoy the moment. I have tucked work areas into armoires and closets that can be closed neatly at the end of the day. Sliding panels are another tool for containing the area.

ERGONOMICS

Whether you're age twenty or eighty, correcting the height of your desk and the position of your keyboard and monitor can prevent headaches, shoulder and back pain, and carpal tunnel syndrome. Start with an ergonomic chair. A consultation with an occupational therapist, who can assess the dimensions and layout of your workspace, is also a worthwhile investment.

SOUND

Sound may be the most individual of all the senses. For me, the sound of my fingers on the keyboard is often enough to increase my energy level. Music may stir you to action. A recording of natural sounds can smooth over distracting noises. Music fed through earphones from a personal music player is also a necessity in shared workspaces to block out distractions.

RITUAL

Establishing routines improves efficiency, even if the routine is not strictly related to the task at hand. Simply knowing where everything is in your space could save you ten minutes each day. A simple ritual such as lighting a candle with a pleasing scent, such as rosemary, cedar, or lemon, can give you an instant boost of energy.

STORAGE

Your filing system, which can include storage boxes, file cabinets, or binders, should have room to expand, but not so much that it encourages hoarding. Switch to paperless statements and billing if it's an option. Take advantage of electronic storage for documents. Leave enough room in a drawer or cabinet for stationery, pens, stamps, and other regular office supplies.

INSPIRATION: MEMORY WALL

PHOTOGRAPHS in frames scattered among different rooms create a crowded feeling that can disturb the sense of sanctuary. Instead, consolidate your favorites; frame them in matching frames or pin images half an inch apart in a cluster that I call a memory wall.

A DEDICATED WORKROOM is a good place for this. Begin in the center of the wall, and let it grow outward. Alternatively, install lean steel or wood shelves in corridors and prop the photos on them; this sturdy horizontal configuration will simplify the presentation. In addition, a shelf provides more flexibility than hanging, and allows you to incorporate tiny objects as well.

TAKE ADVANTAGE OF THE DIGITAL AGE by scanning, labeling, and storing photos on disks. Then you can upload and edit images from family trips and show them on your TV as a slide show for friends and family. I'm also a huge fan of digital picture frames. These devices look like traditional picture frames but they hold images downloaded from your computer or digital camera. You can program them to display the same one picture or a rotating slide show.

OPPOSITE
The sweeping curve of this resin-topped desk widens at one end to create an informal conference table for three or four people. A long-armed task lamp illuminates quiet research, and when used alone, focuses concentration. We use dimmers on all lights, and dim them 5 percent, which makes the bulbs last longer. Art and reference books live in this room on ceiling-height oak and steel bookcases.

SMALL OFFICE AND NOMADIC WORKING

The most important reason for a dedicated workplace is to create a physical space for your mental space. We often squeeze the work area into a small section of another room. Follow these measurements to create a space that is both efficient and comfortable, even if it is small. Surface height should be 28 ½ inches; surface width at least 30 inches. Clearance from the back of a chair to the nearest wall should be three feet. The minimum knee clearance from side to side is 24 inches. It is important that the seat of the chair be adjustable.

A four-inch-thick, eleven-foot-long slab of cream-colored concrete forms a minimal desk that coordinates nicely with the brick wall surrounding my personal home office (see photograph on opposite page). Sunlight streams through a bank of windows, offering contemplative views to the outdoors. Even though nature is in plain sight, I keep two of my favorite orchids at my the desk for added biophilia. Nearby, I have a twelfth-century cowbell and gong bowl from a Buddhist monastery.

As computers get smaller and more portable, and business is done more on a paperless basis, there may seem to be less need for a separate office space. For effortless nomadic working, make your home wireless. Or, if you have a common room kitchen island, install an outlet so that you can plug your computer in and work or surf the Internet while your dinner is cooking or your partner is making coffee.

FOLLOWING PAGES

Left (page 156): This home office doubles as a bedroom, so portable furniture is a must. A desk with casters can be rolled aside to make room for a flip-down Murphy bed (not pictured). Sliding glass doors fill one wall of the room, so when the homeowner desires, he can position the desk and chair (ergonomically tailored for a tall person) in front of them to take in the views. The hanging light fixture is actually an antique felting sieve from a hat factory.

Right (page 157): A handsome slab of cherry wood with an exposed-grain edge forms the desk in this light-filled home office. The work surface contains only the essentials—a lamp, a laptop, a personal organizer—creating a clutter-free environment. Although the office is clearly high-tech, the use of wireless technology prevents a tangle of cords from disturbing the serenity.

(pages 158–159): This warm multifunction workspace looks out over the coming and goings of boats on the East River in New York City. The owner can work at the long, natural-edged desktop or curl up on the sofa bed to watch a movie. A rocking chair and an ottoman invite her husband to come in to chat. The wooden ottomans function as both footstools and tables.

For me, outdoor spaces are simply extensions of the home. I love to bring the inside out and the outside in, staging elaborate meals on the patio, for example, or designing window-walled sunrooms that are basically gardens with roofs. By blurring the line between your home and its surroundings, you'll take advantage of the positive healing powers of the natural world. And your home will not feel like an escape from nature, but rather an intrinsic part of it.

GROWING, CONNECTING, PARTYING

Think about what you love to do in the yard and garden. For some, there's no greater joy than tending a vegetable patch. Others envision grilling and lounging with close friends until dusk. And some people may view the patch of green beyond their window as the scene of morning meditation.

Once you've decided what functions your landscape will serve, use furniture and plant dividers to create discrete areas for different activities, from dining outdoors to growing fresh food for the meals you serve there. The process is really no different than planning an interior room. You should also think about the earth itself as a movable, malleable medium, like a giant slab of Play-Doh™: mound up a grass hill for your kids to roll down, for example, or dig a conversation pit lined with stone benches that can be piled high with pillows.

Let the garden tickle your senses, whether you're indoors or out. Consider planting an aromatherapy garden filled with herbs and redolent flowers near the windows, so that its delightful fragrance will drift through to the indoors. As for sound, the trickle of water is soothing to many, so it's nice to add some sort of water element, such as a fountain or a Japanese koi pond with a miniature, pump-powered waterfall. I like to sit in the morning in a garden in upstate New York listening to the quiet splash of water in a fountain tumbling over basalt pebbles. Or, lying in bed, I can open a window and let the call of a blue jay or the babble of starlings light up my morning. It's the perfect start to the day.

PREVIOUS PAGE
This outdoor living room is steps from the bustling streets of New York City, but it's as peaceful and serene as any sanctuary in nature. A steady gush of water from a stone fountain muffles the sounds of the city. Teak furniture from Sutherland and cushions upholstered with waterproof material from Perennials provide comfortable, weather-resistant seating for dining or lounging in the open air.

OPPOSITE
A pavilion-enclosed terrace on a contemporary loft provides inspiring views of the city and a spot for the homeowner to take a snooze or read the paper. The metal framework doubles as an arbor for clambering green vines that, in time, will have dappled light spilling onto the peaceful outdoor retreat. The railing is raised to meet building code and to create a sense of security that's essential to any sanctuary.

FOLLOWING PAGES
On the same terrace a teak pavilion provides shade for comfortable low-slung seating during the day. At night, its canopy acts as a projection screen for videos, turning the terrace into an exterior media room. The video projector is hidden in the stone-filled trough in the center, which also contains LED candles that flicker brightly no matter how strong the wind. All the materials on the terrace were chosen to withstand the weather, including the small concrete and steel tables.

OUTDOOR ESSENTIALS

PRIVACY

Concealing yourself in the outdoors is a delicious activity. Lattice screens laced with climbing plants or a seating area in a grove of trees can provide places of cover. In the same way that half-on clothes can be sexier than full nudity, half hiding (for example, where a waist-high hedgerow partially conceals an al fresco dining area) can feel more private than total concealment.

PLANTINGS

Whether your green space consists of rolling acres or a few square feet, be mindful of what you cultivate. Non-native plants need more attention, water, and fertilizer. Be clear on what you want to do with plantings in your green space: eat from them, gaze at them, play in them, or maintain them. Consulting with a nursery is informative and usually free.

WATER

If you live in an area where water is plentiful and you have the space, add a reflecting pool with a fountain and colored lights, or build a swimming pool for morning laps. And don't forget the birdbath: the intimacy of watching birds performing their cleansing ritual is irresistible. Similarly, koi ponds with skimming dragonflies provide endless theater.

TEXTURE

Cleverly layered perennials, evergreens, and deciduous trees and flowers create depth and dimension. A scarlet maple is a haiku in the fall against dark yews, while a tulip heralds spring. Use abundance and frolicking plants for the growing season and minimalism for the dormant season. Birch trunks in winter and a lawn party of delphiniums and peonies in summer spell seasonal pleasure.

FOOD PREPARATION

It is a good idea to do your food prep in the indoor kitchen. For the outdoor kitchen, I like built-in barbecues over rolling grills. I work with native materials; for example, sandstone in the Southwest or fieldstone in the Northwest, which I combine with stainless steel so you can clean off the drips.

PETS

Take your animals into account when planning an outdoor space, and avoid plants that are toxic to them. It's great to be able to fling open a door and have a pet rush out to relieve its little furry body. Train your dog to go in a special place, to keep the area clear of unpleasant surprises. Cats, bless them, tend to bury the evidence.

MAINTENANCE

Some people love to *fooster* (a great Irish word that means to putter) in their gardens. Others prefer as little upkeep as possible. This is a big decision: ask yourself if you really want to spend your weekend digging and mulching, or just gazing at a gravel patio and ornamental grasses. If maintenance is appealing, use environmentally sound bug repellants and fertilizers.

MEETING

Outdoor meetings spur creativity and fun. Picnic tables encourage intimacy: they hearken back to childhood. Even the most important mogul loosens his collar when confronted with a picnic of organic grilled vegetables, crusty bread, and a carafe of wine. Make sure your outdoor dining area has adequate seating for a large group, and provides shelter for guests who may be sensitive to sunlight.

STORAGE

A tiny shed or simply a drawer for tools will get you in the habit of storing your garden gear. Keep the storage capacity to a minimum to prevent the acquisition of unnecessary equipment. Labeled tool pegs or a pegboard are excellent organizers. If your house has room for a small greenhouse, it's a wonderful way to turn gardening into a year-round pursuit.

WINDOWS AND WATER

WINDOW TREATMENTS should further the connection between interior spaces and the outside world. A solar shade filters out unwanted rays. Blackout shades protect the home theater from unwanted light and induce sleep in a bedroom. Screened porches can expand the perceived scale of a living room. Shutters will protect the interior from storms and intense heat, and threads of light creeping through the slats will create lovely shadow patterns on the floor.

OTHER PEOPLE'S WINDOWS reveal the values of those who live on the other side. I love to visit Amsterdam, where indoor life is shared through enormous unveiled windows: in the evening as the lights are switched on, pedestrians and cyclists can peek into contemporary Dutch interiors along the canals. In country villages in Ireland, the lace curtains through which one can peer in but not out tell a story. The shutters in Spanish villages close tightly for the night with the inhabitants tucked safely and privately within. French windows wisped with sheers will invite you outdoors on a clement day and evoke a gracious past.

WATER IS THE PROVIDER OF LIFE. Experiment with various kinds of water inside and outside your home. A waterfall or a fountain can help drown out the urban buzz with a splendid splash. Water need not be present on so grand a scale: a large pot full of water becomes a dramatic home for papyrus, and a hollowed-out stone filled with freshwater and gerbera daisies makes an arresting art installation by the front entry. A reflecting pool lined with shiny black granite need not be more than four inches deep to imply a thought-provoking abyss; at times, the surface will bring the earth and sky together. A small pond can house a family of fish, giving you endless fun as you feed them and watch their silky swirls in the water.

OPPOSITE
This fixed glass window in a corridor turns a glimpse of wildlife in a protected marshland into a living artwork. A reflecting pool doubles the visual impact. Water flowing over into a tank amplifies the joyous sound of water falling.

NINE DETAILS FOR CREATING A PERFECT OUTDOOR SANCTUARY

■ Place potted plants or a vase of fresh-cut flowers on your outdoor dining table.

■ Build a tree house for children (or yourself) to hide in.

■ Plant a tree for every member of your household, and a memorial bush or tree for the ones who have passed away.

■ Tend indigenous plants that do not require horrific amounts of water and chemicals to survive.

■ Create water recovery systems to capture the rain and recycle household water for irrigation.

■ Plant fruit trees, both espalier trained and freestanding; they're low maintenance and have a high-edible yield.

■ If there is space, build a pool pavilion housing a toilet, sink, shower, and a small kitchen. It might house a sardine can of

children sleeping on the mattresses from the chaises, or provide shelter from sudden storms for party revelers.

■ Hire an expert to maintain your green space—there is no reason to feel guilty about getting help with your yard work.

■ Plant greens such as thyme and moss between pavers; they will release their scent when stepped on.

OPPOSITE
In a copper-toned corten-steel planter, ornamental grasses wave under a row of young birch trees. An outdoor mirror runs the length of the wall behind the metal planter, amplifying the greenery and bouncing light back onto the terrace. When the birches drop their foliage, their trunks reflect artfully in the mirror, along with views of the surrounding cityscape.

FOLLOWING PAGES
Left, clockwise, from top left: Contrasting shapes provide visual stimulation. A Buddha sits quietly against the stone wall surrounding a grove of birch trees. A trough of translucent stones illuminated from underneath provides light to welcome visitors. Oven-proof black bowls from Colombian potters can be used to float a white flower or to serve a steamy casserole. Water from these spouts pound down to massage the tired shoulders of guests in the warm outdoor whirlpool beneath them. Right: A moon window in a wooded retreat radiates biophilia, or the ameliorative effect of nature on the human mind, body, and soul. Like a secret portal, the window captures a view of a stone garden planted with mosses and irises whose small white flowers glow like holograms at dusk. The window is framed in cold-rolled steel, which from the interior creates an interesting contrast of geometric shapes. When night falls low exterior lighting defines the outdoor space, a feng shui way to create a sense of safety and enclosure.

OPPOSITE

A house perched on a rock formation above a small lake in Connecticut echoes the owner's love of everything Japanese. Evergreens and mosses and a collection of interesting plants have been planted with love and care to create views from the inside. Stone pathways curl around the house and moss creates a silent carpet. The result is a great exercise in good feng shui.

FOLLOWING PAGES

With its wall of windows, this lakeside retreat is as magical as a tree house. In the morning, it's the perfect place to sip coffee, read the paper, and watch the swans on the water below. Come nightfall, the family gathers around the wooden table, uncorks a bottle of wine or two, and enjoys an evening of board games or conversation.

175

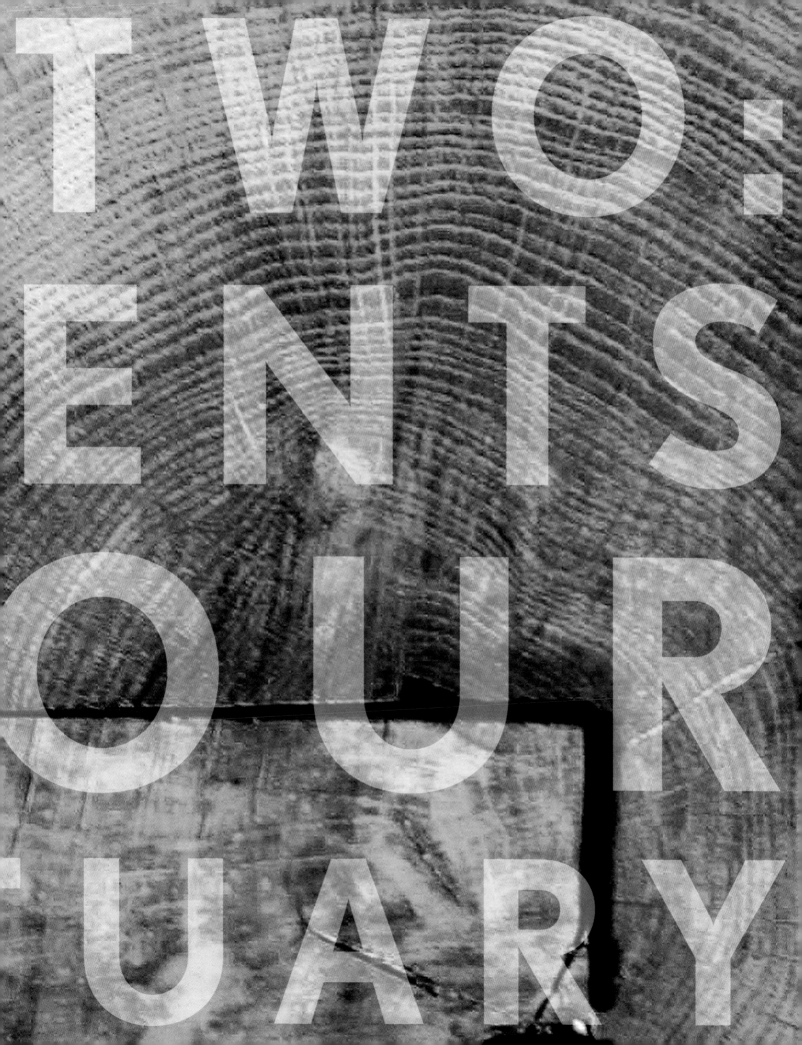

ENHANCING, EVOKING, ENERGIZING

Color is primal. It is instinctive. Even at the age of three, you probably knew what your favorite colors were, yet standing before a fan of paint chips can all but paralyze an ordinarily decisive person. Somewhere along the way, many of us lose touch with our own instinctive reaction to color, but believe me when I tell you that this preference for one color, and aversion to another, is a direct reflection of what you need to achieve balance. Relax and listen to yourself. It is there, touching off light shows of emotion: red for passion, white for purity, green for balance, and so on through the spectrum. You just need to learn how to tap into these colorful hubs of energy.

Chromatherapy is the formal study of the relationship between color and energy. It is an ancient discipline and has been practiced in places like China, India, and Egypt for thousands of years. Chromatherapists (you might also hear them called color therapists) use gemstones, fabrics, candles, and other color tools to deliver physical and spiritual balance. In doing so, they rely on the seven *chakras* of the body, wheels of energy according to various philosophies including Hinduism and Buddhism that are in constant rotation. Each *chakra—muladhara* (red), *svadhisthana* (orange), *manipura* (yellow), *anahata* (green), *vissudha* (blue), *ajna* (indigo), and *sahasrara* (violet)—is associated with a different color. In the home, color can be put to use in much the same way. Its presence determines the mood and energy of a room, indicating places of rest, work, play, and creation—basically each of the areas of the home discussed in the first half of this book.

OPPOSITE
A rest on a teak stool with your back against this Chinese red artisan plaster wall is energizing. The color is so vivid that it reflects red light into adjacent white walls in a great example of how bounced light can infuse a room with an ethereal tint.

COLOR ESSENTIALS

RED

Red seduces. It's aligned with the root *chakra, muladhara,* located at the base of the spine. The root *chakra* enriches all the senses. Red has a stimulating effect, making it a perfect accent color in a dining room—crimson upholstery, for example, or terra-cotta flooring. In the bedroom, jolts of red can stir passion. Be cautious when using this hue as it may affect your sleep.

ORANGE

Orange is aligned with the second *chakra, svadhisthana,* and is often referred to as the belly *chakra,* as it is located just above the navel. Nourishing the soul, this warm hue also energizes and invigorates, evoking creativity and self-confidence. In a common room, it promotes communication. A fireplace is a natural source of orange. You can incorporate hits of the color with an accent pillow or throw.

YELLOW

Yellow belongs to the third *chakra, manipura,* known as the solar plexus. It elevates mood and alleviates exhaustion. Its proximity to the stomach helps with digestion, making yellow an appropriate color in the kitchen. Paint one wall a soft creamy hue, or add bright yellow towels or tableware. Yellow is not good in a bedroom, as it keeps the mind revving.

GREEN

Green is harmony. It's associated with the fourth *chakra, anahata,* often called the heart *chakra* because of its location near that vital organ. Green is a cool color and an excellent balancer. It encourages healing and restoration. It is a wonderful color in bathrooms and bedrooms. Green also promotes tolerance and understanding.

BLUE

Blue is aligned with the fifth *chakra, vissudha,* located in the "V" of the collarbone. It is the color of communication, engendering lightness and peace. This makes it a good choice for common rooms, as it expands the space. The calming effects of blue induce sleep, so it can be used as an accent in the bedroom. But too much blue can cause melancholia.

INDIGO

Indigo is the color of divine knowledge and spirituality. Aligned with *ajna,* the sixth *chakra* in the forehead, indigo fosters intuition. Indigo and brown work beautifully together as brown grounds this *chakra.* Indigo is often the color of the night sky, which invites the brain to make sense of our existence. Given the cerebral aspect of indigo, it is suited to studies and libraries.

VIOLET

The color violet is aligned with the seventh *chakra, sahasrara,* which is often referred to as the crown, since it is located just above the skull. Violet is a regal color, associated with passion and motivation. It brings higher understanding and calm and enhances the soul's purpose. These qualities make violet an excellent choice for the bedroom or meditation room.

BLACK AND WHITE

White is not associated with any one *chakra.* Instead, it is the yang from which all colors spring. Too much white can feel sterile, but when applied properly it coveys cleanliness and vibrancy. Black is the ying that absorbs all the colors. Used sparingly, for example in the base of an accent lamp or in the frames of photographs, it promotes balance.

BROWN

Brown shares an association with the root *chakra.* However, its energy is geared more toward stability and weight. Too much brown can provoke depression, but when applied thoughtfully, brown inspires elegance and reassurance. It's ideal for a study, perhaps in the form of a heavy wooden desk. It can also do wonders in a living room, for example in a chocolate-colored sofa.

NATURAL COLOR

In a sense, all colors are natural, as they all are found in nature. However, we have come to associate browns, grays, and muted greens and golds with the term "natural." A room can be built up by layering textures: stone, woven wool and silk rugs, straw-colored plaster containing straw pieces, and layers of clay and smoky graphite. If you choose a neutral palette for a room, make sure to use lots of textures for visual impact. A walnut floor with a natural wool rug highlighted with splashes of bone silk or hemp will provide a good ground. Add a hefty slubbed linen for a sofa and an unfinished edge to a massive coffee table. For light, a glowing paper Noguchi lamp will bind everything together. Indigo, umber, and poppy red accents can be splashed onto the space in the form of a chenille blanket and overscale pillows.

Many of the materials that I rely on in my designs use neutral palettes that contain other hues: for example, a slate floor contains flecks of blues, ambers, and ochres. Some neutral-toned textiles are woven with brightly colored threads.

OPPOSITE
Neutral color palettes are easy on the mind, without being dull. In this dining area, muted blues and grays set a soothing tone for entertaining. The upholstery on the bench and chair is a deep blue, like something from the bottom of the sea. It plays well with the warm, honey hues of the wooden table and bench frame. The amber glow of incandescent light filters through a handmade paper fixture on the far wall.

COLOR SHIFTS AND CONTRASTS

It is important to remember that colors change with the context. A stone wall may look golden in the morning light, and lilac by dusk. This shift is delightful and keeps us in the present. The red hue of a large carpet in a wheat-colored room reflects differently than a flaming-red poppy placed in front of a brilliant indigo wall. Consider the colors in the context of your home, your sanctuary. Take inspiration from the ideas in this chapter, using them as a creative guide, but also follow the instincts of your *chakras*. Color is a state of mind. The energy you draw from it—supportive, soothing, or energizing—is the measure of its value.

Bounced light is basically light reflected from a colored surface and kissing adjacent surfaces with some of this color; for example, afternoon sunshine blasts light at a large red painting in my loft, which then blasts back red reflections all over my floors and the adjoining walls. Color can be bounced in many ways. Mirrors and crystals are good feng shui tools for refracting and bouncing light as well as energy. A small fountain with a spotlight aimed at the water will send light ripples over walls and floor. Sunlight through waving leaves just outside the window creates stimulating shadow play on an interior wall.

OPPOSITE
Color and light are inextricable, and so the application of color in the home must always take into account the presence of light. This woven lattice light fixture glows orange when illuminated, casting shadows onto the nearby wall and ceilings. Orange stimulates communication, so a fixture like this belongs in a common area dedicated to socializing.

FOLLOWING PAGES
Left: Never underestimate the power of white to transform a space. After all, it's the yang from which all other colors emerge. In this whimsical tableau, porcelain vases on ebonized bases conduct a comedic conversation above a resin bowl the color of pond water. Natural light from a nearby window creates an arresting feng shui shadow play out of the curious arrangement of organic shapes.

Right: Contrasting colors give the eye a place to rest. Make sure it will be a stimulating stopover by reserving the effect for meaningful features in the room. A found object, such as this polychromatic wooden cow head from Mexico, is a suitable candidate. Not only is it a visually invigorating artifact, it serves as a reminder of a glorious road trip taken by the owner. In this sense, its value surpasses the most expensive piece of artwork.

LISTENING, HEARING, SILENCE

Sound is the most individual of the senses. Consider music, with its infinite nuances and themes, each appealing to a different ear. There's bluegrass and bossa nova, classical and jazz. And music is just one of the many manifestations of sound. Chanting is sound. Laughter is sound. And the natural world serves up a blessed abundance, from trickling water to whistling wind and the awesome clap of thunder. Each sound is unique, as is the response they evoke in us.

We fill our homes with sound like we fill them with furniture. Because sound is not visible, however, people aren't always as deliberate in their selection. Try not to make this mistake. Think carefully about the sounds that will identify your home, whether it's the chime that greets visitors who ring your doorbell, the music you play, or the external sounds you either block out or let in. Speaking of sound control, you may need to consult with an acoustical engineer if you live in a house with thin floors and floorboards that can act like tuning forks and magnify unwanted sounds. Avoid positioning your bedroom under or above the kids' rooms, as your play and their play won't necessarily make good acoustical companions. Keep a range of recordings in your entertainment center—music, nature, meditative, and more—for different moods. Digital music players, such as iPods, make it easy to store a virtually endless supply of recordings; with wireless speakers or a portable dock, you can play them anywhere in the home. Lastly, don't forget about the absence of sound. Create places of perfect stillness throughout the home, for example in your workspace or meditation spot, where you'll connect with the rhythms of your breathing and beating heart, or what Simon and Garfunkel called the "sounds of silence."

OPPOSITE
This thirty-six-foot concrete ledge can seat twenty listeners as the owner sings and plays her custom bronzed piano. To capture good feng shui energy in the living room of a high-rise apartment, a reflective Robert Lee Morris sculpture was placed on the concrete ledge.

FOLLOWING PAGES
(page 194): Even a simple shower provides the opportunity to let yourself float in the moment. Listening to the sound of water, whether in a shower, running into a wash-basin, whooshing in a dishwasher, or filling a pasta pot, links us to an elemental human state. (page 195): A shower of natural crystals tinkles when they touch in a breeze. These are set in a corner, capturing good *chi* and dispersing it throughout this home.

SOUND AND SILENCE ESSENTIALS

BELLS, SINGING BOWLS, GONGS

Bells dispel stale *chi*. Once a week walk around your home with a bell in hand and ring it in every corner to disperse the stagnant energy. I use a twelfth-century cattle bell from Thailand and a centuries-old Buddhist temple bowl gong. Both instruments resonate beautifully and effectively. Coupled with burning incense, chimes recharge a home's energy in a matter of minutes.

NATURAL SOUNDS

One of the great pleasures of meditation is capturing and parsing different sounds. Take a moment to focus on the sound of birdsong or the rain hitting your window. Define a quiet space, preferably near a window or door that can be opened wide during temperate weather to let in the sounds of nature or the neighborhood.

SURFACES

Surfaces greatly affect sound. In a room with walls and ceilings covered in drywall, plaster, tile, or stone, sound waves bounce around like a ball in a squash court. Even if you have a spare aesthetic, some textiles, soft furniture, rugs, and carpets are necessary to absorb sound waves. Acoustical paneling, textured walls, and slatted window treatments will also help to soften sound.

SOUNDPROOFING

Creating a totally soundproof room is expensive, but there are easy ways to muffle the noise. Place a closet on the wall between neighboring bedrooms to create a buffer. In the bathroom, an exhaust fan will drown out noises. If you're remodeling, consider investing in soundproof drywall and double-glazed windows—two panes of glass with a space between them that functions as a sound insulator.

MAKING MUSIC

Making music is one of the most joyful family activities. Basic piano- or guitar-playing skills will encourage the release of joy. Every home should have an instrument, preferably in the common room where family and friends most often gather. You need to let sound out once in a while, even if it is just by belting out show tunes in the shower.

SOUNDS AND SCENTS

White noise machines and recordings of nature induce sleep without filling the mind with chatter. Be selective in your choice of sounds. The pitter-patter of rainfall is more uniform than the sound of the roiling sea. Soothing sounds work best when paired with pleasing scents; for example, lavender oil.

CHIMES

A set of wind chimes hanging outside a kitchen window will send positive energy into the home. At a garden gate or front entry, chimes can alert you to approaching visitors. When choosing chimes, listen carefully; each note is unique, so you want one that touches the right frequency in your body. Look for an alarm clock with a chime mode.

RECORDINGS AND SCENTS

Even if your home isn't wired with surround sound, personal music players make it easy to set a different aural tone in every room. As a counterpoint to music, recordings of natural sounds are available online. They can lull you to sleep, or can link an urban space to nature. A recording of water is a way to bring that element into a room.

VOICE

Our own voices are naturally healing. Releasing sound from the body creates cleansing vibrations and is an energy-detox that calms the chattering monkey mind. Like dissipating waves in a still reflecting pool, as you release sound, you establish calm, healing sound waves that are picked up elsewhere throughout your body, connecting energy channels.

RECHARGING, REJUVENATING, HEALING, THRIVING

Wellness is a state of mind, a feeling from within. But it is promoted by the energy of our surroundings. Given that most of us spend more time at home than anywhere else, this is the environment that has the greatest impact on our mental and spiritual well-being. In this sense, our homes define us as individuals. If they are cluttered and chaotic, we're likely to be stressed out and high-strung. Alternatively, a home that is clean, orderly, and rejuvenating—a sanctuary in the truest sense of the word—will instill balance, harmony, and joy in its occupants. In this chapter, I discuss some of the elements that I consider essential to promoting wellness. Not all of them pertain directly to home design, but they'll all make your home a more restorative place.

Wellness is also habitual. It may seem strange to think that you can get into the habit of feeling good. But it's absolutely true, and it's through the making of our homes that we establish healthy routines. If your refrigerator is stocked with fresh vegetables, your diet will be healthy. If a corner of the common room is dedicated to meditation, you'll make this therapeutic activity part of your daily routine. If the home is filled with light and candles, your body will respond to the warmth and good humor.

OPPOSITE
Peopled by quiet footfalls and the trickling of a small fountain, or brightened by sound from hidden speakers if the mood strikes, the benches here invite passersby to sit for a moment of contemplation. Stripes of light splash patterns through a slatted exterior wall to stretch an ever-changing runner along the corridor.

FOLLOWING PAGES
(page 200) In this truly spa-inspired master bath, a glass-enclosed shower stall has room for two and a luxurious rain-style showerhead that's like standing in a warm, tropical downpour. Placing a handsome trough with arching orchids on the edge of the vanity nearest the toilet enhances the sense of privacy even more. Natural stone tile work throughout the bathroom has a calming effect.

(page 201) Combining natural and artificial light sources engages multiple senses at once. In this arrangement, a stack of recessed fixtures on a slatted wall provides visual rhythm. A scented candle on a steel ledge augments the soft illumination while filling the area with its healing fragrance.

WELLNESS ESSENTIALS

FITNESS

The ritual of returning to the same spot in your home for a daily workout will help condition your mind and body. It doesn't require an entire room. Dedicate one corner of the common area to fitness. Four of my favorite portable pieces of equipment are a small indoor trampoline, an exercise ball, a stationary bike, and a yoga mat.

A QUIET PLACE

Designate a spot for chanting, prayer, or simple reflection. It may be a cushion in a corner on which you can sit cross-legged, or a swath of floor—six by eight feet should be large enough—where you can roll out a yoga mat. Meditation and prayer can be mobile, too—they can be practiced in the back garden, for example.

SPA TREATMENTS

The hands-on exchange of energy one receives during a massage lingers long after the treatment ends. In addition to visiting offsite spas, it is possible to incorporate areas for home treatment into a bathroom, bedroom, or concealed outdoor space. Enhance the environment with special aromatherapy candles, soothing music, or natural sounds, and a strict phone-free policy.

LIGHT

Light is a mood enhancer, and it is one of the best ways to achieve balance and harmony. It can be applied in various ways. Windows and skylights let natural light into the home. Fireplaces and candles bring in the light-generating element of fire. Beam lights up toward your ceilings to transform dark corners, or light candles to bring in positive feng shui.

EXTREME LIVING

Live life as if you will some day die. An enormous selection of joys is available to us but we sometimes shut down and do nothing at all. An organized, supportive home makes spontaneous living possible. If you've designed the perfect kitchen, have an impromptu dinner party. Or, luxuriate all day in a calming bedroom. Seize each day.

CLEANSING

This concept applies equally to the home and the body. Just as you cleanse your storage of unused, out-of-fashion things, and purge your filing cabinets quarterly, adopt the same sort of routine for your body. The skin is a good place to start. A weekly visit to the sauna will keep your skin silky and your pores clean. Discuss fasting with a nutritionist before trying it.

TIME MANAGEMENT

Stress is wasted energy. Time management is the antidote, and all it requires is a little forethought. At the start of each day, make a list of what you want to accomplish. Stick to it, and don't add new tasks if you hit your goals early. Use the found time to relax. In the kitchen, keep the pantry stocked with supplies for last-minute meals.

FOOD AND DIET

Look into your refrigerator and pantry. Do the items there support healthy living? Is your counter piled high with fresh fruit? I believe strongly in eating local and organic food. Potted herbs in a window box provide both year-round. As water is essential to well being, install a powerful water filter under your kitchen sink.

COMMUNICATION

Choose comfortable furniture and arrange it in a social manner: side-by-side seating can be as intimate as chairs that face one another. Think about the close quarters in a car, where you're not eye-to-eye with your companion. As orange is the color of communication, it should be included in gathering spaces in the form of painted surfaces, flowers, or furnishings such as pillows.

GLOSSARY: A TOOLBOX

This glossary provides explanations of the terms and phrases that have helped define my role as a designer, which is to create healthy, sustainable environments where families can live, work, relax, and play. These are the tools that my designers and I reach for most frequently in our studio. They're the modalities that inform my work, the words that provoke my thinking. I should point out that I'm not an expert in these fields, but I rely on people who are, whether it's a feng shui master or a biogeometrist, as readily as I do engineers or AV consultants.

This integrative approach is essential to my philosophy as a designer. We all share the same light and energy, and we breathe the same air. By sharing these terms with you, I hope we'll also be able to speak the same language in relation to designing the home as your sanctuary. Although the terms cover a wide range of disciplines, from ancient mysticism to the latest government-led initiatives in energy efficiency, they're united by what I call the four S's of sanctuary living: Sustainable, Sensual, Sexy, and Serene. Every conversation I have with a client or member of my design team relates in some way to these core values, and the same can be said for the terms that follow. I've briefly explained what each one means to me, and have provided a reading list on page 222 for further study. Worthwhile reference Websites are included.

OPPOSITE
Hallways function as passageways through the home, but they're also opportunities for unexpected hits of drama. In this long, somewhat awkward corridor, a wooden, polychromatic Buddha resides in an angled niche, adding a sense of calm and order. Proper lighting is a critical part of designing a corridor. Here, a light at the end of the hallway subliminally draws people to one end, enhancing the energy flow and making the rooms off it feel more engaging.

FOLLOWING PAGES
(page 207) Clockwise, from top left : The graceful hand of a Buddha radiates peace and stillness. Movement circulates *chi* in this two-way mirrored art lamp; warm light moves from one box to the next, momentarily illuminating it—and erasing its reflective properties. A shoes-off household gives the people who live there and visit the tactile pleasure of the floor surfaces on the soles of their feet. A lantern provides a silent welcome when the owners arrive home after work or travel.

(page 211) Clockwise, from top left: An acacia tree reveals its ancient heart in this detail of a hand-polished thirty-inch-diameter wooden ball. Cylindrical tables topped with cast concrete are a good place to display finds from recent travels or rest a coffee cup. A fire bowl on a hilltop terrace beckons owners and guests for storytelling or stargazing. To welcome visitors, an expanse of sky is captured and doubled in this still reflecting pool outside the entry door.

AROMATHERAPY

I'll never forget driving through New Zealand when I rounded a corner and came down a hill into a plain totally covered with lavender. I opened the window to inhale the fragrance, which delivered instant calm and happiness. The sense of smell is a great tool for enhancing moods and healing the human body. Every aroma affects different nerve centers of the body and evokes various emotions—from the sexy, soothing warmth of *ylang-ylang* to the pure wake-up call of lemon thyme and mint. When designing a space, I'm keenly aware of the way aromas will contribute to the overall feeling. You should avoid scents you find unpleasant.

ASTROLOGY

As far back as I can remember I've been checking people's horoscope signs and looking at how they relate to the characteristics of my own, Libra. If you are a member of a team, or if you are flummoxed by your spouse, the knowledge of a person's astrological sign will give you quiet insight into his or her inner workings.

BIOGEOMETRY

Biogeometry is related to feng shui. It is the study of the effect physical shapes have on energy fields and, in turn, on the human body. Dr. Ibrahim Karim, an Egyptian, has been a leader in this field for more than forty years. He has shown how energy lines emanating from the earth are measurable, and how sometimes these lines can cross in ways that have injurious consequences to health. Such crisscrossing can be corrected with the use of magnets and colors, and through the alteration of the shapes of rooms, furnishings, and more.

BIOPHILIA

The literal translation of this term is "love of life or living systems." Harvard University entomologist Edward O. Wilson, the father of biophilia, believed that humans have a genetic affinity for nature. In studies supporting this philosophy, patients who were exposed to greenery or other scenes of nature had faster recovery rates than those who were not. A flash of green grass through the window, a wall covered by vines, a basil plant in your kitchen window—scenes like these in the home contribute to the healing effects of nature on the human spirit.

CHAKRA

The term *chakra* refers to energy forces associated with colors that run through our body. Each "energy" color contains specific properties that affect a person's emotional, mental, and spiritual wellbeing. Red is aligned with the first *chakra, muladhara.* This hot color represents life energy, physical strength, and vitality. Orange is associated with the second *chakra, svadhisthana.* It is a warm color that energizes, invigorates, and nourishes. Yellow is connected to the third *chakra, manipura.* This vibrant color can stimulate the nervous system and affect emotions. Green is associated with the fourth *chakra, anahata.* A cool color, green is a great balancer. The fifth *chakra, vissudha,* is aligned with blue. It is the color of communication and peace. The sixth *chakra, ajna,* is connected to indigo. This color builds a positive outlook and brings inner-strength. Violet is aligned with the seventh *chakra, sahasrara.* A regal hue (also known as the color of inner-power), violet brings higher understanding and calm. It is a great color for mediation spaces.

CHROMATHERAPY

Also known as color therapy, chromatherapy is a form of alternative medicine in which color and light are used to influence the mood and energy of a room. Chromatherapists rely on a variety of tools and materials in their treatments, including light, candles, gemstones, and dyed fabrics. The seven main colors are red, orange, yellow, green, blue, indigo, and violet, and they correspond to the seven *chakras* of the body. Yellow, for example, corresponds to the third *chakra,* the solar plexus, and might be used to enhance the body's metabolism. For more information on color, see page 181..

CRITICAL PATH

This is a technique for planning projects that identifies interdependent key tasks. It is often used for large construction projects, but I've included this term here because I've found it useful in completing small and medium-size tasks as well. When creating a sanctuary, it is common to get snagged in an old habit or frustration. Outlining a critical path will help you to see the project with clarity and create reasonable expectations; for example, organizing your closet is more difficult if you don't first schedule two to four hours alone without interruptions. A tough-minded friend can help you edit and dispose of your castoffs.

ELEMENTS

The Chinese identify five elements: earth, water, fire, wood, and metal. Each of these elements has a different energy, and they relate to each other in a continuous cycle of creation and destruction: wood fuels fire, fire makes earth (ash), earth bears metal, metal collects fire and water, water nourishes wood; wood parts earth, earth absorbs water, water douses fire, fire melts metal and burns wood, metal chops wood. In an ideal home setting, these five elements will be in perfect balance; for example, fire could be symbolized by candles, water by an aquarium or fountain, earth by bricks, wood by furniture, and metal by silverware. When designing a room, it's important to make sure that one element doesn't dominate, or the energy will be off-kilter; for example, if there's an abundance of metal in a room, it will start to feel dangerous. Adding a water element will balance the energy, since water weakens metal by causing it to rust and decompose.

EXPERTS

Rely on people who devote themselves to a subject and master it. There are some you may only need once but whose expertise will save you a great deal of hassle down the line, such as an architect, a designer, a feng shui master, or mechanical engineer. There are others you might turn to when you least expect it.

Keep a list of these top ten expert consultants in a kitchen drawer. This list might include a cleaner, plumber, electrician, air-conditioning technician, computer repair person, and contractor. The Internet and phone book are fine places to look for experts, although word of mouth is often the most reliable resource.

FENG SHUI

Feng shui is the Chinese art of positioning buildings and organizing interior spaces to create a positive energy flow, or *chi*. Feng shui is both practical and spiritual. It is not design, per se, but it informs design by promoting harmony, health, and prosperity in the lives and work of the occupants. During the last twenty-five years, my studio has used a feng shui master on almost all our projects. Where we have not, we have followed the precepts of feng shui to guide us in the creation of life-enhancing spaces. This includes everything from choosing colors that energize a space to removing the clutter that inevitably leads to stagnant *chi*.

HERBALISM

This traditional form of medicine is based on the healing properties of plants and plant extracts. The use of herbs to treat illnesses and disease is timeless and universal. The Romans did it, as did the ancient Chinese and the Native Americans. It would be foolish not to do the same, even if it's something as simple as drinking peppermint tea to relieve an upset stomach. There are many herbal remedies out there worth exploring.

LAUGHTER YOGA

Dr. Madan Kataria, an Indian doctor and student of yoga, established the laughter movement in 1995. He calls it "nature's stressbuster . . . it lifts our spirits with a happy high that makes us feel good and improves our behavior towards others." He also notes that laughing with others is a great way to build bridges and promote peace in the community. There are now over six thousand laughter clubs all over the world. To find one near you go to http://www.laughteryoga.org.

LEED

Short for Leadership in Energy and Environmental Design, LEED is a green-building certification program launched by the U.S. Green Building Council. For a building to earn LEED certification, it must satisfy various criteria covering water conservation, materials selection, sustainable site development, and more. At a minimum, a LEED-certified building must be 15 to 20 percent more energy efficient than a conventional one. For more information, including advice on where to find green professionals, visit The U.S. Green Building Council at www.usgbc.org.

LOHAS

This acronym stands for Lifestyle of Health and Sustainability. It refers to the companies that provide socially responsible, ethical, and environmentally sustainable products and services, and the consumers who purchase them. Since it was founded in 2000, the LOHAS market has grown into more than a two-hundred-billion-dollar industry, with approximately thirty-five million "LOHAsians" in the United States alone. I definitely count myself among them. For more information, visit www.lohas.com.

PALIMPSEST

This is another word that seems to fit in with my pleasure of *wabi-sabi*. Palimpsest refers to documents where words have been scraped off and new words have been written over them. This is interesting for me because I believe it describes the way I work. I use references to the past, but always partially delete or alter them; in so doing, I move our work deeply into the twenty-first century. I delete and scrape away stagnant and stale ideas, and useless information, and I use the wisdom of the past to inform new projects.

RENEWABLE ENERGY

Renewable energy is in perpetual supply unlike carbon-based energy, which can only be used once and then is gone—except for the emissions it releases into the atmosphere. Some common examples of renewable sources are wind, solar, and geothermal. Not only are these energy sources renewable, they are a lot cleaner and safer than coal or nuclear-generated energy. In most states, it is now possible to buy renewable power through your local supplier. To learn more, visit The Green Power Network, a division of the U.S. Department's of Energy's Office of Energy Efficiency and Renewable Energy at www.eere.energy.gov/greenpower. For a guide to cutting back on energy usage in the home, go to www.saveonenergy.com.

SAD SYNDROME

Seasonal affective disorder occurs as the nights get longer and daylight is gone by the time you finish work. You can replace sunlight with full-spectrum light in your home. A body clock will awaken you with a slow light, like the sun coming up. A big lightbox in your home will increase your body's melatonin levels, which in turn will improve your mood. I get the seasonal blues and trick myself into thinking it is summer by shining my reading light down on my face after the alarm goes off in the morning; the heat and light sift through my eyelids and I can feel the energy rising.

SEX

I am putting sex in this glossary because I design bedrooms and other spaces, like garden areas, where you can have great sensual moments. Kissing and massage as well as sex itself benefit from intentional design in various spots in the home. I put a love light—simply a very dim, soothing fixture that can be turned on to create a romantic ambience—in every bedroom so that you can unveil yourself to an amber rosy glow. A candle or a dimmable fixture works fine too. Bring generous, blanket-size towels with you for nomadic sex on your sofa, or place a soft rug in front of a roaring fire for a comfortable spot. When designing a new home, I try to place the adults' rooms away from the children's rooms so that parental play doesn't interfere with that of the kids.

SUSTAINABILITY

Sustainability is for real. In the simplest terms, it is about living in a way that has the smallest possible impact, or footprint, on Mother Earth. Buying only local and organic food is an example of sustainability. Planting native trees and shrubs around your home that thrive on available water is another. Be mindful of bringing furniture into the home that is made in accordance with fair trade laws and made of eco-friendly materials. All of these practices are easy to adopt, and they will all go far toward making the planet safe and wonderful for future generations.

VASTU SHASTRA

This ancient science is a close relative of feng shui, so I often find myself using them in conjunction. *Vastu shastra* deals with the planning and building of living environments so that they are in harmony with the surrounding energies. There are four main elements of *vastu shastra*: site, structure, movable objects, and furniture. It applies from the planning phase of a project right through the selection and placement of the furnishings.

VOCS

Volatile organic compounds, or VOCs, are solvents that are emitted as gases from a variety of household products, including paints, cleaning supplies, and building materials. According to the Environmental Protection Agency, VOCs cause acute symptoms such as asthma, headaches, dizziness, and throat irritation. Some of the solvents are also believed to be carcinogens. Look for low or no-VOC products to use in your home; for example, many paints now come with little or no VOCs. By referring to the label, you can usually find out exactly what goes into a product.

WABI-SABI

In my opinion, the Japanese have one of the most aesthetically refined cultures in the world. *Wabi-sabi* is their word for the celebration and reverence of the natural aging of both objects and creatures: an imperfect glaze on a sake cup is revered; an ancient artisan is called a national treasure. *Wabi-sabi* implies humble, simple things, like an ancient spoon whose stains have united to create a patina. A faded Kilim on a reclaimed wide board floor implies the Zen acceptance that the new will eventually acquire a patina and become *wabi-sabi*. I love to interfere with surfaces with acids and washes and hammers or other tools to create instant *wabi-sabi*, as it is sometimes hard to wait. A good patina can be achieved in a day, so you can either bring old objects into the home or distress new ones.

WATER THERAPY

Water is an essential life force, like air, sunlight, and sleep. Our bodies are composed of approximately 70 percent water on days when we are well hydrated. Both the sound of water and the sight of clean water are cleansing to the body and soul. There are so many wonderful ways to incorporate water into the home and garden, whether it be a gurgling fountain, a koi pond, or just a clear vase or pitcher filled with filtered water. After a stress-filled day, before you hop into bed, stand in the shower for a minute: water washes away bad energy.

WIRELESS

Going wireless is fairly simple for the home computer user. According to technical expert Rob Pillartz, you will find devices for most personal computing functions, from keyboards and mice, to networking and printing. For a person living in a small apartment where space is at a premium, wireless printing is an extremely attractive option. Not only does it reduce cable clutter, it also frees you to place your printer virtually anywhere in your home. Make sure to check compatibility before buying any wireless equipment as not all wireless adapters work with every computer or printer. A good technical consultant or knowledgeable salesperson should be able to help you make the right purchase.

GREEN CLEANING

Creating a healthy environment in your home and garden includes making sure that everything you clean with or compost is handled in a biodegradable and soil-enhancing manner. Not long ago, white vinegar, lemon, and baking soda were used to clean everything in the house—from the kitchen counters to the tub. An effective way to clean is with a combination of hydrogen peroxide and vinegar sprayed on separately (test a small hidden area first). Lemon juice and salt combine to make a grainy but nonabrasive pan cleaner. These homemade cleansers are now joined by a host of cleaning products that work well without being hard on the environment. The practice of using chemical-free cleaning products not only improves indoor air quality but has a minimal impact on the environment. Such companies as AMF, Dr. Bronner, Harmony, Gaiam, Ecover, and Seventh Generation often have the benefit of being sustainably manufactured and have recyclable and biodegradable packaging. Buy natural-bristle brushes, natural cleaning sponges and cloths, and remember to rinse your cleaning items before putting them away.

OPPOSITE
These decorative copper bowls from Colombia are individually handcrafted by gypsies. Their reflective interior is tin. They are not only great as foot bowls for your home spa but can be used as water vessels for cleaning. You can also serve fruit in them.

CLOD
CHC

AGH'S

OICE

I have had the fortune of working with the best and brightest in every field of design and wellness—from artisans and consultants to spiritual healers. I collect these experts the way some people gather fabric swatches or furniture pieces. Rather than keep my sources secreted away, I believe in sharing them with kindred spirits. If you have read this far, I would say you are one of us. I hope you will benefit as much from the following sources as I have.

Throughout the years I have been invited by companies to design products ranging from textiles and accessories to lamps and chairs. Many of these Clodagh Signature licensee's products are available through the Clodagh Collection showroom. They are marked with the Clodagh logo below.

Clodagh Collection
670 Broadway, 4th floor
New York, New York 10012
(212) 780-5307
www.clodagh.com

ACCESSORIES

ANTIQUARIUS
at Clodagh Collection

APF MUNN
MASTER FRAMEMAKERS
60 Fullerton Avenue
Yonkers, New York 10704
(914) 665-5400
www.apfgroup.com
Clodagh Signature licensee

ASIAPHILE
825 Western Avenue, #15
Glendale, California 91202
(818) 550-1450
www.asiaphile.com
Clodagh Signature licensee

MARTHA STURDY
16 West Fifth Avenue
Vancouver, British Columbia V5Y 1H5
(604) 872-5205
www.marthasturdy.com

NORMA KAMALI
11 West 56th Street
New York, New York 10022
(212) 957-9797
www.normakamalicollection.com

ROSEMARY HALLGARTEN
at Clodagh Collection

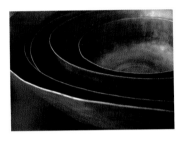

SUREVOLUTION
at Clodagh Collection
Clodagh Signature licensee

ART

CHRISTOPHE RAYNAL
at Clodagh Collection

ELENA COLOMBO
342 Park Avenue
Brooklyn, New York 11205
(718) 399-2233
www.firefeatures.com

ESPEN EIBORG
at Clodagh Collection

HANAFUSA
at Clodagh Collection

LOUISE CRANDELL
at Clodagh Collection

MERJA WINQVIST
at Clodagh Collection

PETER O'KENNEDY
at Clodagh Collection

SIOBHAN McDONALD
at Clodagh Collection

CARPETS

AM COLLECTIONS
584 Broadway, 2nd floor
New York, New York 10012
(212) 625-2616
www.amcollections.com

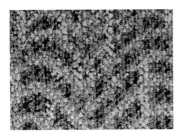

BENTLEY PRINCE STREET INC.
14641 East Don Julian Road
City of Industry, California 91746
(800) 423-4709
www.bentleyprincestreet.com
Clodagh Signature licensee

TUFENKIAN ARTISAN CARPETS
919 Third Avenue
New York, New York 10022
(800) 432-9917
www.tufenkiancarpets.com
Clodagh Signature licensee

CONCRETE

ROBERT YOUNGER
274 Water Street
New York, New York 10038
(917) 576-9623
Younger33@earthlink.net

CONTRACTORS

DUCE CONSTRUCTION
412 West 127th Street
New York, New York 10027
(212) 316-2400
www.duceconstructioncorp.com

PRO NEW AGE DESIGN
240 East 76th Street
New York, New York 10021
(917) 805-3936

SEASIDE CONSTRUCTION
345B Beach 87th Street
Rockaway, New York 11693
(718) 318-1111

WISE CONSTRUCTION LLC
180 Varick Street, #512
New York, New York 10014
(212) 929-6181
www.wiseconstructionllc.com

FABRICATORS

DELFORM
2255 Highland Cross, Ste. 6
Rutherford, New York 07070
(201) 438-3915
www.delformstudios.com

LA CUISINE INTERIORS LLC
343 Monroe Drive
West Palm Beach, Florida 33405
(561) 655-9550
www.lacuisine-interiors.com

FURNITURE

BENCHMARK FURNITURE
MANUFACTURING
300 Dewitt Avenue
Brooklyn, New York 11236
(718) 257-4707
www.benchmarkfurnituremfg.com

BRENT COMBER
at Clodagh Collection

CHISTA
at Clodagh Collection and
537 Greenwich Street, 6th floor
New York, New York 10013
(212) 924-0394
www.chista.net

DENNIS MILLER ASSOCIATES
200 Lexington Avenue, Ste. 1510
New York, New York 10016
(212) 684-0070
www.dennismiller.com
Clodagh Signature licensee

DOUGLAS THAYER
at Clodagh Collection

JIUN HO
322 Sixth Street, Ste. 6
San Francisco, California 94103
(415) 437-2284
www.jiunho.com

JOHN HOUSHMAND
31 Howard Street
New York, New York 10013
(212) 965-1238
www.johnhoushmand.com

HUDSON FURNITURE
433 West 14th Street, Ste. 2F
New York, New York 10014
(212) 645-7800
www.hudsonfurnitureinc.com

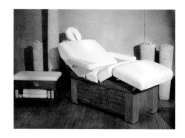

OAKWORKS
923 East Wellspring Road
New Freedom, Pennsylvania 17349
(717) 235-6807
www.oakworks.com
Clodagh Signature licensee

RALPH PUCCI INTERNATIONAL
44 West 18th Street, 12th floor
New York, New York 10011
(212) 633-0452
www.ralphpucci.net

ROTSEN DESIGN
at Clodagh Collection

SUTHERLAND
979 Third Avenue, Ste. 813
New York, New York 10022
(212) 871-9717
www.davidsutherlandshowroom.com

TUCKER ROBBINS
at Clodagh Collection

GLASS

GALAXY
277 Fairfield Road
Fairfield, New Jersey 07004
(973) 575-3440
www.galaxycustom.com

HARDWARE

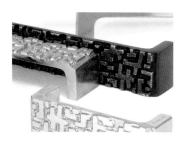

DU VERRE
188 Strachan Avenue
Toronto, Ontario M6J 2S9 Canada
(416) 593-0182
www.duverre.com
Clodagh Signature licensee

KITCHEN AND BATH

ANN SACKS
37 East 18th Street
New York, New York 10003
(212) 529-2800
www.annsacks.com
Clodagh Signature licensee

DEX STUDIOS
Candler Warehouse Lofts
675 Metropolitan Parkway, #1068
Atlanta, Georgia 30310
(404) 753-0600
www.dexstudios.com
Clodagh Signature licensee

KOHLER
444 Highland Drive
Kohler, Wisconsin 53044
(920) 457-4441
www.kohler.com

SUBZERO
P.O. Box 44130
Madison, Wisconsin 53744
(800) 222-7820
www.subzero.com

WATERMARK
350 Dewitt Avenue
Brooklyn, New York 11207
(718) 257-2800
www.watermark-designs.com
Clodagh Signature licensee

~~~~~

WOLF
P.O. Box 44130
Madison, Wisconsin 53744
(800) 332-9513
www.wolf.com

LANDSCAPING

PLANT SPECIALISTS
42-25 Vernon Boulevard
Long Island City, New York 11101
(718) 392-9404
www.plantspecialists.com

TERRAIN-NYC
Steven Tupu
200 Park Avenue South, Ste. 1401
New York, New York 10003
(212) 537-6080
www.terrain-nyc.net

ZONE 6 INC.
David Kulick
589 Broadway, 2nd floor
New York, New York 10012
(212) 219-4070

LIGHTING

DANIEL BERGLUND LIGHTING
141 Grassy Hill Road
Lyme, Connecticut 06371
(212) 243-1718
www.danielberglundlighting.com

BOYD LIGHTING
944 Folsom Street
San Francisco, California 94107
(866) 251-7777
www.boydlighting.com
Clodagh Signature licensee

FLOU
42 Greene Street
New York, New York 10013
(212) 941-9101
www.flou.it

JOHN WIGMORE
at Clodagh Collection and
1265 East Seventh Street
Upland, California 91764
(917) 690-0024

LEO SCARFF
at Clodagh Collection

PAGANI STUDIO
at Clodagh Collection

VISUAL COMFORT
2021 Bingle Road
Houston, Texas 77055
(713) 686-5999
www.visualcomfort.com
Clodagh Signature licensee

~~~~~

LIGHTING DESIGNERS

ANN SCHIFFERS
485 Warburton Avenue
Hastings-on-Hudson, New York 10706
(914) 478-0553
www.annschiffers.com

DESIGN ONE
25 Park Place, 2nd floor
New York, New York 10007
(212) 477-5662
www.designonecorp.com

FOCUS LIGHTING
255 West 101st Street
New York, New York 10025
(212) 865-1565
www.focuslighting.com

G2J DESIGN
226 Kimberly Place
Riverdale, New York 10463
(917) 573-7565
www.g2jdesign.com

HORTON LEES BROGDEN
200 Park Avenue South, #1401
New York, New York 10003
(212) 674-5580
www.hlblighting.com

LINENS

DONNA KARAN HOME
819 Madison Avenue
New York, New York 10021
(212) 861-1001; (800) 231-0884
www.donakaran.com

FRETTE
4 West 58th Street
New York, New York 10019
(800) 353-7388
www.frette.com

HOMESTEAD
1359 Broadway, 17th floor
New York, New York 10018
(646) 839-7043
www.homesteadbrands.com
Clodagh Signature licensee

MATTEO
912 East Third Street
Los Angeles, California 90013
(213) 617-2813
www.matteohome.com

MATERIAL RESOURCES

MATERIAL CONNEXION
127 West 25th Street, 2nd floor
New York, New York 10001
(212) 842-2050
www.materialconnexion.com

METALS

J FREDERICK CONSTRUCTION, INC.
71 Commerce Drive
Brookfield, Connecticut 06804
(203) 740-2907
www.jfrederickconstruction.com

STUDIO DELL'ARTE
74 Bayard Street
Brooklyn, New York 11222
(718) 599-3715

PHOTOGRAPHERS

DANIEL AUBRY
365 First Avenue
New York, New York 10010
(212) 414-0014
www.aubryphoto.com

ERIC LAIGNEL
530 Canal Street, #2E
New York, New York 10013
(917) 204-4338
www.ericlaignel.com

PETER MARGONELLI
6 West 18th Street, 8th floor
New York, New York 10011
(212) 941-0380
www.petermargonelli.com

KEITH SCOTT MORTON
39 West 29th Street, 11th floor
New York, New York 10001
(212) 889-6643
www.keithscottmorton.com

STORAGE

CALIFORNIA CLOSETS
1000 Fourth Street, Ste. 800
San Rafael, California 94901
(800) 274-6754
www.calclosets.com

SURFACES

ART IN CONSTRUCTION
55 Washington Street, Ste. 653
Brooklyn, New York 11201
(718) 222-3874
www.artinconstruction.com

ASHLEY STUDIO
11807 County Hwy. 14
Delhi, New York 13753
(607) 746-7678

BORO PLASTERING INC.
393 Jerico Turnpike, Ste. 206
Mineola, New York 11501
(516) 746-4100
www.boroplastering.com

CASIMER KOWALSKI
P.O. Box 13491
Charleston, South Carolina 29422
(843) 762-6123
www.casimerkowalski.com

WYATT CHILDS, INC.
1598 Johnstonville Road
Barnesville, Georgia 30204
(770) 358-0501
www.wyattchildsinc.com

ICE STONE
Brooklyn Navy Yard
63 Flushing Avenue, Unit 283, Building 12
Brooklyn, New York 11205
(718) 624-4900
www.icestone.biz

ISLAND DIVERSIFIED
4062 Grumman Boulevard, Building 81
Calverton, New York 01933
(631) 953-6990
www.islanddiversified.com

LIGHTBLOCKS
MB Wellington Studio
141 Canal Street, Mill #2
Nashua, New Hampshire 03064
(603) 889-1115
www.lighblocks.com

ROBIN REIGI
48 West 21st Street, Ste. 1002
New York, New York 10010
(212) 924-5558
www.robin-reigi.com

SERPENTINE STUDIO INC.
27 Vestry Street
New York, New York 10013
(212) 674-7235

TECHNOLOGY

ROB PILLARTZ
Technologist
244 Fifth Avenue, Ste. 2455
New York, New York 10001
(212) 252-4589
www.connexxys.com

TEXTILES

LAURA LIENHARD TEXTILES
at Clodagh Collection

MARLA HENDERSON DESIGN
at Clodagh Collection

PERENNIALS OUTDOOR FABRICS
140 Regal Row
Dallas, Texas 75247
(888) 322-4773
www.perennialsfabrics.com
Clodagh Signature licensee

UPHOLSTERY

THE FURNITURE JOINT
35 Great Jones, 2nd floor
New York, New York 10012
(212) 598-4260
www.furniturejoint.com

WOOD, SPRING, AND DOWN LTD.
366 Canal Place
Bronx, New York 10451
(718) 292-1002
www.woodspringdown.com

WELLNESS

ALBERTO AMURA
Environmental Dowser, Biogeometry,
Healer, and Reiki Master-Teacher
(575) 770-1415
www.lighttide.com

CORNELIA SIGNATURE PRODUCT
at Clodagh Collection and
Cornelia Day Resort
663 Fifth Avenue
New York, New York 10022
(212) 871-3050
www.cornelia.com

DR. MADAN KATARIA
Laughter therapy and yoga teacher
www.laughteryoga.org

MIRAVAL LIFE IN BALANCE
5000 East Via Estancia Miraval
Catalina, Arizona 85739
(520) 825-4000
www.miravalresort.com

DR. RUBIN NAIMAN
Sleep Programs, Miraval Resort
5000 East Via Estancia Miraval
Catalina, Arizona 85739
(520) 770-1003

RANCHO LA PUERTA
Deborah Szekely, Founder
Tecate Baja California, Mexico
(800) 443-7565
www.rancholapuerta.com

SARAH ROSSBACH FLEMING
Feng Shui Consultant
102 Ridge Road
Rumson, New Jersey 07760
(732) 741-9545

SPA FINDER, INC.
257 Park Avenue South
New York, New York 10010
(212) 924-6800
www.spafinder.com

DR. ANDREW WEIL
The Weil Foundation
P.O. Box 922
Vail, Arizona 85641
www.drweil.com

WINDOW TREATMENTS

MECHOSHADE
Solar Shading
42-03 35th Street
Long Island City, New York 11101
(718) 729-2020
www.mechoshade.com

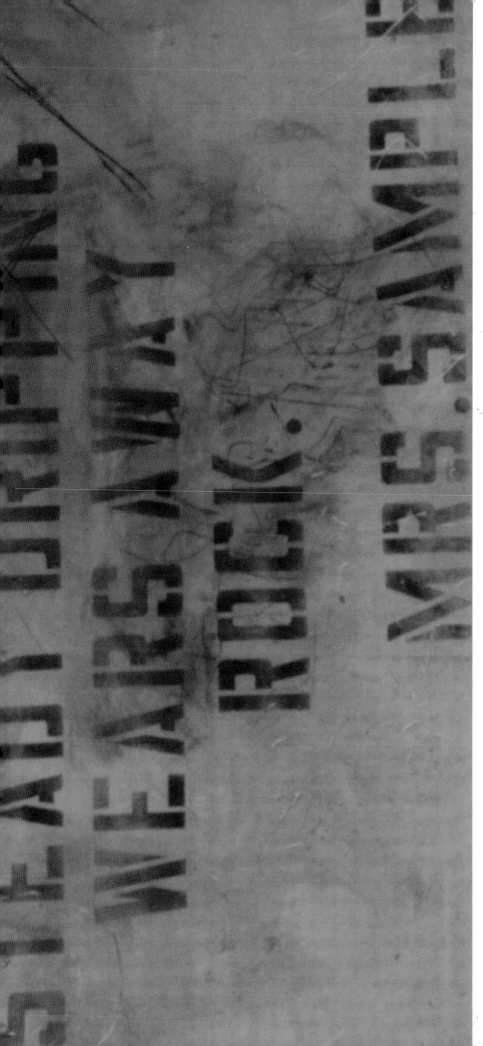

Benyus, Janine M. BioMimicry: *Innovation Inspired by Nature.* New York: HarperCollins Publishers, Inc., 1997.

Beylerian, George M. and Dent, Andrew. *Ultra Materials: How Material Innovation is Changing the World.* New York: Thames and Hudson, 2007.

Davis, Patricia. *Aromatherapy A to Z.* Essex: The C. W. Daniel Company Ltd., 2004.

Emoto, Masaru. *The Hidden Messages in Water.* Hillsboro: Beyond Words Publishing Inc., 2004.

Goodman, Linda. *Sun Signs, How to Really Know Yourself through Astrology.* New York: Bantam Books, 1971.

Hunter, Linda Mason and Halpin, Mikki. *Green Clean: The Environmentally Sound Guide to Cleaning Your Home.* New York: Melcher Media, 2005.

Juracek, Judy. *Surfaces: Visual Research for Artists, Architects, and Designers.* New York: W. W. Norton & Company, Inc., 1996.

Kingston, Karen. *Clear Your Clutter with Feng Shui.* New York: Random House, 1999.

Liao, Sabrina. *Chinese Astrology: Ancient Secrets for Modern Life.* New York: Warner Books, Inc., 2000.

Lipman, M.D., Frank. *Total Renewal: Seven Key Steps to Resilience, Totality, and Long-term Health.* New York: Penguin Group, 2003.

McDonough, William and Braungart, Michael. *Cradle to Cradle.* New York: North Point Press, 2002.

Rossbach, Sarah. *Interior Design with Feng Shui.* New York: Penguin Books, 2000.

Silverman, Sherri. *Vastu: Transcendental Home Design in Harmony with Nature.* Layton: Gibbs Smith, 2007.

Tanizaki, Junichiro. *In Praise of Shadows.* New Haven: Leetes Island Books, 1980.

Weil, M.D., Andrew. *Eight Weeks to Optimum Health.* New York: Time Warner Paperbacks, 2007.

Wilson, Edward O. *Biophilia.* Cambridge: Harvard University Press, 1984.